Stories in Action

Library of Congress Cataloging-in-Publication Data

Gordh, Bill.
  Stories in action : interactive tales and learning activities to promote early literacy / By Bill Gordh.
    p. cm.
  Includes bibliographical references and index.
  ISBN 1-59158-338-1 (pbk : alk. paper)
  1. Storytelling. 2. Early childhood education—Activity programs. I. Title.
  LB1042.G66 2006
  372.67'7—dc22   2006007465

British Library Cataloguing in Publication Data is available.

Library of Congress Catalog Card Number: 2006007465
ISBN: 1-59158-338-1

First published in 2006

Libraries Unlimited, 88 Post Road West, Westport, CT 06881
A Member of the Greenwood Publishing Group, Inc.
www.lu.com

Printed in the United States of America

The paper used in this book complies with the
Permanent Paper Standard issued by the National
Information Standards Organization (Z39.48–1984).

10 9 8 7 6 5 4 3 2 1

*For my mother, Gwen Gordh, my wife Jenny, and my two children,
Cody and Rachel, and for all the children who have heard
or will hear these stories and make them their own.*

Contents

Part One:
Exploring Themes through Stories

Part Two:
Exploring Character through Stories

**Part Four:
Exploring Structures of Stories**

Acknowledgments

I want to acknowledge and thank the following people and institutions: The Episcopal School in the City of New York (with Directors Dick Davis, Carole Lembo, Cheryl Kelly, and currently Judith Blanton and Curriculum Directors Cathy Smith, Jane Charry, and currently Jiffy Noble) where all this work began and continues and which awarded me a summer writing grant to complete this manuscript. I thank Principal Allysa Pollack and the parents and students at PS 150 (TLC) in Tribeca, New York City, where I have had an annual Storytelling Residency since 1999; Executive Director Jackie Pine and Early Stages where the "Using Folktale Story Structures as Models for Creative Writing" continues to develop with PS 203 (Principal Carole Nussbaum), PS 41 (Principal Terri Graybow and my lunch group of teachers); and other public schools in New York City, Manhattanville College where I co-direct a Summer Arts Institute with Dr. Patricia Vardin and Christine Mulligan (Shelley Wepner, Dean) and the following individuals who have suggested picture books to augment the materials in each chapter: Marilyn Iarusso, Rita Auerbach, Christine Mulligan, and the students in the Manhattanville Summer Arts Institute 2005. I also want to thank my editor, Barbara Ittner, who has helped me fashion this work into what I hope is a useful and inspiring book.

Introduction

Stories in Action brings you a selection of stories and activities to share with children from early childhood through early elementary. But this is more than a story and game collection. This book represents years of working with and refining stories to engage children in meaningful early-literacy-based activities that whet their appetites for joining the wondrous world of reading and writing and telling stories. Building listening, sequencing, and predicting skills; developing memory strategies and imaginative solutions; and supporting increased understanding of story structure all contribute to the emergence of early literacy. The stories and activities in this book support the development of all these important skills.

How you use the material in this book depends on your relationship with the children. How many are in your group? How old are they? Are they talkative? Is English their first language? How often will you see them? These are just a few of the many variables that no book can amply address, but I hope this volume will provide the support and ideas you need to do your best work.

Building Early Literacy

The stories and activities in this book support reading readiness for the prereader and help build skills for the early reader. Reading these stories to children will engage them, and the activities that follow will enhance literacy skills. But actively enacting and telling the finger plays and telling the other stories directly to the children will elicit their participation in ways that reading cannot accomplish. Storytelling engages the children directly with the words of the narrative. There are simply three elements: you, the listener, and the story. The children sense the special quality of this immediacy and become more engaged than when there's a book they can look at or refer to later. From where you sit, the children become the object of your narration. You also do not have a book to refer to, and so the immediacy is formed in both directions. (This is not to belittle the importance of reading to children but rather to point out some of the unique benefits of telling stories.) Telling a tale sets up a situation in which the story can be adjusted to the circumstances. By following the suggested methods of telling the tales, you will engage the young listener in building his or her understanding of story, a skill that will help in the world of reading and writing. The activities that follow the stories are fun for the children and provide the spark to ignite the joy they can experience by reading a good book. *Stories in Action* supports the growth of these important early literacy skills:

- Listening skills

- Sequencing skills

- Predicting skills

- Narrative skills

- Vocabulary building

- Oral expression and expressiveness

- Observation skills

- Understanding Story Structures

- Understanding stories through physical involvement: acting out stories, finger plays

- Building strategies for retelling

- Observing similarities and differences in stories

- Building comprehension

  - Phonological awareness

  - Vocabulary

  - Print awareness

  - Print motivation

Literacy Connections are made throughout the book. They point out how the stories and activities support the growth of skills and understanding related to literacy. The Literacy Connections appear following the words **Literacy Connection**.

The Stories in This Book

Folktales are central to this book. The tales included (other than a few original stories) represent stories from cultures all around the world. The stories are nonviolent and were chosen to present a wide range of male and female characters. These tales have been told from generation to generation, and many have traveled around the world, changing as they go to suit the culture and teller who is telling them. They continue to transform for me as I tell them from year to year. They change when I flash on a new way to engage a child with a sound or a word. They change when a young listener joins in on a chant or asks a question that changes how I understand the story. They change for smaller and larger groups, for older and younger children.

Here they are captured in print for you to use, but I hope they will not remain as they are. Tell these stories and watch them change as you learn how they work for you and what you want to accomplish through them. The folktales are rich in characters and in meaning. They offer a glimpse of the culture they represent. There's a reason they have been around for a long time, and that is that they are tales of people's feelings, thoughts, experiences, and imaginations. This book is an enjoyable collection of tales, but more important, it is a resource for you to use to create many, many illuminating experiences for children.

I have titled the book *Stories in Action* because the stories presented are for active involvement of the child listeners. These tales are "in action!" in a variety of ways. The opening story of each chapter is "in action" because the tale is retold as a finger play. Taking the finger play notion from simple story-songs like "Five Little Ducks," I have selected fifteen folktales from around the world that lend themselves to be retold in a simple way. By adding easy-to-do hand and finger gestures to accompany the tales, the children are excited to join in on the telling by copying the gestures of the teller. The finger plays are "stories in action." But there are more than finger play folktales in this book. In fact, in addition to the fifteen finger plays, there are twenty-seven more stories.

These additional stories expand on the theme introduced by the opening finger play in each chapter. Not all stories lend themselves to becoming wonderful finger plays, but this does not diminish their power or usefulness in the process of building early literacy skills. They offer other opportunities. Stories can be "in action" in many ways. Some involve the children by asking them to echo or join in on a refrain. Some of the stories were written to be retold for acting out. Others set up games or story-making activities. Still others are for active listening and for building pure listening skills. Forming these relationships with the tales makes the children active participants in developing their understanding of how stories work. The boys and girls help build their own prereading and early-literacy skills.

Finger Plays As Literacy Launch Pads

Finger plays delight young children who generally join in with just the simplest of invitations. They become pathways for them to find out more about stories and how they are structured; you can use these finger plays to set up a wide range of story making and story-related activities. Each chapter in *Stories in Action* begins with a finger play. Following the finger play, other stories and activities further the understanding of the exciting premise of the chapter. The finger plays, originally appearing in *15 Easy Folktale Fingerplays* (Scholastic, 1997), become launch pads for exploring story structures, themes, and cultures. The book also provides models and resources to expand on the work that is offered. The stories are wonderful tales that any age group will enjoy. When the activities lend themselves to a specific age group, they are so noted.

The book is not sequential. Each chapter stands on its own, and you can start with any chapter depending on the kind of exploration you are guiding.

Organization of the Book

Stories in Action is divided into four parts:

Part One: Exploring Themes through Stories

Part Two: Exploring Character through Stories

Part Three: Exploring Cultures through Stories

Part Four: Exploring Structures of Stories

Each part has one or more chapters illuminating the overall subject of that part. Each chapter takes one aspect of the subject and explores it through the stories and activities presented.

Part One: Exploring Themes through Stories

Using stories to animate an exploration of any theme is a good way to involve children of all ages. Stories can illustrate an idea, set up a game, and provide a circumstance for children to explore the idea through dramatic play. Often after hearing and participating in these stories and activities, children begin seeing thematic connections to other stories and events. They also see how themes affect the choices they make in the creation of stories. These chapters support the building of observation skills that will lead them to notice thematic elements that tie literature together.

Part Two: Exploring Character through Stories

Part Two consists of one chapter focusing on one character: the trickster spider found in many West African tales. Following one character through many stories enriches each of the stories. The character gains depth, and the listener gains understanding of the character by observing his behavior in a variety of circumstances rather than with a series of descriptive terms like *greedy* or *lazy*. This exploration becomes a model for the study of other story characters. (For instance, there are a couple of American Indian Coyote Tales—Chapters 3 and 8—that can be expanded into a character study of Coyote.) Part Two contains stories and activities for all ages.

Part Three: Exploring Cultures through Stories

The three chapters in Part Three use folktales to take a glimpse at several cultures. Mexico, the Amazon, and Northeast Woodlands America provide vibrant tales sure to engage every boy and girl. The stories motivate children to find out more about these places and peoples. The stories do not try to be the defining tales of a people, because that is truly an impossible task; rather, they provide an adventurous journey for young listeners and story participants. The activities are more literacy based than culture based but will further any investigation you may be doing. Although an in-depth study of a culture is probably not on the agenda for the younger children, these stories and activities (as marked) are wonderful to share with any age group.

Part Four: Exploring Structures of Stories

Chapters 11 through 14 are devoted to structures of stories. The *study* of the structure of stories is aimed at the older children (second, third, and fourth graders), but younger children will enjoy the tales as well. In fact, sharing these stories with pre-K, kindergarten, and first graders exposes children to the structures that they can examine more methodically in future years. There are also specific pre-K through first-grade activities sprinkled throughout Part Four. For early elementary, the tales become models for the children to create their own stories.

How This Work Was Developed

I began working in early childhood at The Episcopal School in New York City in 1987. The Director of Curriculum invited me to initiate story explorations with some of the classes. These generally consisted of the children creating a story sequentially with each child adding to the story. We then started acting out stories. The children became animated in a wondrous way I had not encountered before. I began looking for more stories to use with the children. I discovered the wonder of folktales and the additional multicultural benefits of sharing stories from around the world. I found that it usually took reading through at least fifty stories to find one that was just right for these young children. I kept reading and sharing stories. In 2004–2005, as Director of Expressive Arts, I told 150 stories from all over the world from a list of more than 250 stories that I have developed into interactive tales to use with young children.

As I retold these tales, I noticed how the children were taking in the stories and began altering the way I told them to accommodate their learning. Soon the tales had short refrains in which the children could join, and the patterns in the stories were emphasized with rhythms and pauses. The stories suggested games that would allow the children to take their story experience to another exciting place. Incorporating words in the stories that the children used in the games that followed enriched their vocabularies. I discovered that by creating a story with a description of a game's action, children then have a more meaningful experience with the game. A story followed by activity also strengthens their sequencing skills. This work with early childhood continues to grow.

My work at Episcopal School is three days a week, so I use my other days to explore beyond early childhood. The skills the early childhood students brought to their next grades led other schools to invite me to develop work with their classes. My published writing, public performances, and workshops led to a yearly residency (beginning in 1999) at Tribeca Learning Center, a public school in New York City, creating storytelling curriculum for pre-K, kindergarten, and first through fourth grades.

The work with story structures presented in Part Four was developed in early elementary classes through Early Stages, a New York City arts organization. Working closely with the executive director, Jacqueline Pine, we developed the prototype for the organization's Storytelling Residency programs in New York City Public Schools. Jackie saw the possibilities for storytelling to pave the way for young students to become better readers and writers. Using folktale structures as models for the students' creations is the central feature in the second- and third-grade residency program. Many of the finger plays in this book have become "Take-Home Tales" in the Early Stages program. The Take-Home Tales, a term coined by Ms. Pine, are stories the students take home and tell their families. By using finger plays, the children remember the gestures and use their own words to tell the tales.

As luck would have it, the pilot school for this program was PS 203 in Queens, New York, where the principal, Carole Nussbaum, recognized the potential of the program. I got to work closely with the school's librarian, Jane Aaron, who helped me refine the work as we progressed. After working and playing with the structures of the stories presented in Part Four, the students began noticing how these structures combine and appear in many forms of literature. *Understanding the structure of a story helps children predict and gain an understanding of how a story works, empowering them to analyze and feel in control of the reading, writing, and speaking they are called on to do.*

The Chapter Elements

There are fourteen chapters of stories and activities in this book, and although they explore different themes, they are similarly organized. Each chapter basically works like this:

- Brief chapter introduction

- Finger play warm-up

- The Finger Play: The story that launches the chapter's exploration

- Storytelling tips for the finger play

- Activities based on the finger play

- Additional Stories: One or more stories (mostly world folktales) to further the exploration of the chapter's theme

- Storytelling tips for the additional stories

- Activities based on the stories

- Story Skeleton: A one-page outline of each of the additional stories to be used for retelling the tale

- Picture book references: A list of picture books that also explore the focus of the chapter

- **LITERACY CONNECTIONS** are made throughout the book.

Here is a bit more about the chapter elements.

The Finger Plays

Kinds of Finger Plays

Finger play is a diverse and flexible way to tell stories. Here are some of the types of finger plays you'll find in this book:

- Some finger plays represent characters: the shape and movement of the hand and fingers represent different characters, such as Spider, Rabbit, or Sun.

- Some finger plays depict the reader or storyteller as a character: in *The Tomorrow Monkeys* and *The Stonecutter,* for example, the storyteller becomes a character, and the hands represent other elements of the story.

- Some finger plays describe movement: rain falling (fingers wiggling downward) or characters walking (hands patting thighs) are examples of this kind of finger play. Sometimes the finger play describes the action of the characters rather than the characters themselves. For example, in *Sparrow and Crow,* the sparrow asks the woodcutter to chop down the tree. Instead of representing the woodcutter as a finger character, the finger play suggests his action—chopping.

Finger Play Warm-Up

 Each time you lead a finger play, you should start with a warm-up for the fingers. This gets the fingers of the children moving and makes the girls and boys aware that you're inviting them to participate physically in the telling of the tale. This warm-up is designated in the text with the icon seen here.

Note that this symbol appears in the beginning of each chapter just before the finger play. If there is additional warming up to do specific to the story, it is noted following the basic warm-up icon

Basic Finger Play Warm-Up: Have the children echo your finger movements. By doing the warm-up in silence the children focus on the movement. Then when you tell the story, they can expand their focus to include listening and watching and copying the finger play. The amount of time you spend on the warm-up, and the speed at which you do it, depend on the children's age.

Have the children physically echo the following actions:

1. Hold up one finger. Wiggle it around.

2. Hold up two fingers. Wiggle them around.

3. Hold up three, then four, then five fingers, wiggling them around.

4. Add the fingers from the other hand.

5. Move hands in a wave.

6. Move hands up and down.

7. Place hands in your lap before you begin the finger play story so that the children do the same and are ready to listen. Then they join in with your hand movement when it is introduced in the story.

Finger Play Warm-Up Variations: There are many variations on the finger play warm-up to keep the children engaged. These include the following:

- Change the speed of your fingers as they move.

- Begin the warm-up with left hand sometimes and with right other times.

- Start with a different finger or with a different number of fingers.

- Add sounds to the finger moves.

- Allow a child to lead warm-up.

General Tips for Sharing Finger Play Stories

The finger plays that open each chapter are quite simple to do. The movement of the fingers works much the same way as in the toddler finger plays "Where Is Thumbkin?" and "Five Little Ducks," but the story content is considerably more complex. Nonetheless, these finger plays, based on folktales, have been whittled down to basic narrative elements. In this simplified story form, they can be illustrated and enjoyed with simple finger and hand gestures. Each finger play in the book has illustrations that suggest the finger play to accompany the story. Portions of the text are in bold to show where the gestures should begin.

To demonstrate the ease of using these stories and the fun you can have with children, here's a great little folktale from Ghana, West Africa, that has been turned into a finger play. It incorporates the African "Call-and-Response" (echo) to teach the children the story while echoing the finger play. As you will find in the rest of the book, a dialogue follows as a model for yours with the children.

Bill: Let's begin with a finger warm-up. Now watch what my finger does and copy it. Ready? [Cup your hand around your ear to indicate that you are listening for their response. If they don't say anything, let them know what you want, "If you're ready, say, 'Ready!' "]

Children: Ready!

[Lead the finger play warm-up described earlier.]

Bill: Now, we're ready for the story. In this tale from West Africa, the fingers are talking. Put up your little finger like this [hold up your little finger].

Children: [They hold up their little fingers.]

Bill: The fingers are talking, and you can echo me as I speak for each finger.

Why Thumb Lives Apart from the Other Fingers (West Africa)

[Hold up one finger at a time starting with small finger. Have thumb tucked. Children echo vocally and with their fingers.]

Leader:	**Echo:**
1. I'm Hungry.	I'm Hungry.
2. Why don't you cook?	Why don't you cook?
3, I'm the tallest!	I'm the tallest!
4. Hey, now, look!	Hey, now, look!
We're talking food	We're talking food
Not size!	Not size!

REPEAT twice more.

[Wiggle 4 fingers while making arguing noise]

Leader:	**Echo:**
AWRRAARA!	AWRRAARA!

[Move thumb]

Thumb says	Thumb says
Too much fuss, Too much fight	Too much fuss, Too much fight
See you later	See you later
Good Night!	Good Night!
BOING! [Move thumb from fingers]	BOING! [Move thumb from fingers]

And ever since the thumb has lived apart from the quarreling fingers!

The End

Storytelling Tips for "Why Thumb Lives Apart from the Other Fingers"

Everyone loves learning this story. It's simple and clever. You can teach it just as it is presented here. However, here are some additional ideas that might make it more exciting for you or the children with whom you work. You may want to use a different voice for each finger. After a few tellings, older children can tell this story to others—at home, in class, or in an assembly. Recently some pre-K children have asked to act it out. Several children played each of the fingers and thumb. They stood in separate places and echoed me. The thumb echoed its part and then moved away from the fingers. They loved it, and the story was even more meaningful and memorable for them.

The finger play stories in this volume have been set up so that you do not really "teach" them to children, in the sense of sitting down and going over the gestures beforehand and then practicing them. The finger plays are naturally inviting to children. Once you have asked them to join you with one finger character, they will look for opportunities to join you as you tell the tale. They can't wait to participate! Following along with the gestures will complement their listening to the tale. You may want to start with the shorter stories, but as you and the children get accustomed to the finger plays, the long ones will be a fun challenge. Specific storytelling tips and some ideas for elaborating the finger play follow each story.

Here are a few more general tips to pave the way.

- On your own, read the story aloud a couple of times before sharing it with your children. Practice the finger play as you read so it becomes natural. **The text in bold** indicates when the illustrated finger play takes place. When you share the story as a finger play, you will see that the children perceive using the gestures as totally natural. So if you need encouragement, just get one of these finger plays going with the children. You'll quickly see how much fun they are for everyone!

- If you use the book when you first "tell" the story, introduce it to the children and show them the pictures of the finger play. They will be ready to join in. Chances are, they will suggest you bring out the book again!

- If you decide to "tell" the story instead of reading it, practice reading it aloud and doing the gestures a few times. Then tell the story in your own words using the finger play to remind you of the structure. Just like the children, we remember better when gesture accompanies the tale. Our hands remember the stories.

- As you introduce a new gesture, you can pause for the children to join in, but not for too long because you don't want to stop the flow of the narrative. These are stories the children will want to do many times, and gestures they missed the first go round can be picked up on one of the retellings. Because I wanted to keep the finger plays simple and inviting, illustrations are included for a basic successful telling with children. Many of the tales work wonderfully with many more gestures, however. Suggestions for additional gestures follow many of the stories. These are ones to have fun and play with, and you may come up with gestures that make more sense to you or that are especially fun for your children. They often remember something new (a phrase, gesture, or sound) that is added spontaneously. It has an extra spark and they appreciate and remember that. These are your stories; let them work for you.

The Other Stories

In each chapter following the illustrated finger play and related activities, you will find more wonderful stories that continue the chapter's focus. These stories are generally more complex than the finger plays and can be read or (better still) told. Storytelling tips follow the stories to offer suggestions on making the particular story effective and to put the tale "in action." Most of the storytelling tips can be used in some form for any story you tell. The story skeleton (described later) can be used when retelling the tale, so that you can make it your own. All the stories in the book use simple language and were written to be told—thus the repetition and rhymes. These tales are from many cultures and are appropriate for listeners of any age. The activities have been built more specifically for a specific age group (early childhood and/or early elementary).

Story Activities

You will find a variety of activities created specifically from the stories and chapter focus. Each activity is described in detail following the story from which it grew. One activity, Acting Out Stories, appears many times because it allows children to be part of the structure of the story. By acting out stories, they begin to understand these structures from the inside out. Perhaps even more important, they love this activity! The activity of "Acting Out a Story" follows the same basic format from story to story. Following are some general guidelines for this activity. When appropriate, there are story-specific activity additions following the story.

Some Tips for Acting out Stories

Acting out a story is a wonderful way for children to understand the structure of a given tale. The young children experience the structure; the older children can experience *and* discuss the structure. Their understanding occurs by being part of the tale and experiencing how their character works in the whole story. There are very few (if any!) stories that children cannot successfully act out. I have often thought that a story, because of its characters or actions, could not be acted out, only to be persuaded by a group of four-year-olds to give it a try. It always works, and it is always amazing! Here are some tips:

- Acting out stories is a children-only activity. Sometimes it may seem simpler for you or another adult to be one of the characters (such as a mother or a father), but it is important that the children have the world of the story for themselves. They find the emotions and attitudes to be any of the characters that are needed, and every story they act out makes them more cohesive as a group. On a rare occasion, you may decide to be part of a story and such cases are noted in the activity section following a particular tale.

- Gather the children. Read or tell the story while they sit before you. Use an area that has some empty space around you.

- Tell the children that they can act out the story.

- Once they have heard the story and have been told they can act it out, the boys and girls are likely to start yelling out the characters they want to be.

- Once the dust has settled, say, "Now I'll name all the characters and point [to spots in the room around the "acting out space"] where that character stands. If you are thinking of a character I forgot, just stay here, and we'll find you a spot."

- The flexibility of using the story skeleton for retelling allows you to include more or fewer particular characters for the acting out activity. For example: "Now, if you want to be Turtle, stand over there. Two of you want to be Turtle? OK, I'll retell the story with two turtles." Another way to alter a story to accommodate a child is to have a brother and a sister in a story that only mentions a girl, or a grandpa instead of a grandmother, or a puppy instead of a dog.

- When you have named all the characters, if someone is left, ask her or him what character he or she is thinking of. Give the character a spot on the side of the performing space. Children may pick up on a character you might not think of. I once had a girl who wanted to be the aromatic steam that came from the stew and enticed Spider to come and taste it (see *Spider's Stew Cap* in Chapter 7). It was marvelous how she danced the part around the room, and I would never have thought of the steam as a character. Many stories have incidental characters or objects that we don't tend to notice. But the children do, and they are telling you how they found a way to be part of the activity. Other surprising character choices have included a carrot, a rock, a tree, a dungeon, and a storm. These all came about by leaving an open space for their ideas. Given the opportunity, children often dazzle you with their unique perspective.

- Retell the tale as the children act it out using the characters that they have chosen. The "Story Skeleton" (see the next section) is handy for retelling the tale because it gives you the basics of the story. Sometimes children remember the dialogue or make up their own. Sometimes they wait for you to supply the dialogue. Either way works. Flexibility is the key, so take your cues from the children. As you become accustomed to telling stories while they are acted out, you will learn to "read" the children and follow their impulses in a creative, supportive and productive way. The retelling demonstrates the flexibility of these stories. By hearing the story retold to accommodate the acting out, children become aware of the different parts of the tale. They discover *what can and cannot change* without altering the meaning of the story. These are good skills to develop for their burgeoning literacy.

There are three rules for acting out stories:

1. Listen to the storyteller. ("So you can hear what happens in the story. Remember, sometimes it may change a bit from the first time you heard it.")

2. Be safe! ("Be careful with your body making sure you and your friends are safe.")

3. Have fun!

For quick reference, here's a summary outline for acting out stories:

A. Tell the story.

B. Name characters and point to spots around the "Acting-Out Space" where the children playing those characters should stand.

C. Ask remaining children what characters they noticed in the story that they would like to be. Designate spots for them to stand.

D. Remind everyone of the three rules.

E. Retell the story as the children act it out.

The Story Skeleton

Each of the stories that is not a finger play in this book has a story skeleton printed on a single reproducible page. The skeleton gives the basic sequence of characters and events without the embellishments. It is the bones of the story, and you can flesh it out with your own descriptive words. The skeleton allows you to be more flexible with the story, a crucial element when retelling for children to act out. The skeleton also allows you to focus or expand on one part of the story. It allows you to add description and movement to a character that a child has picked that was barely mentioned in the original. The skeleton sets you up to tell the story in three or fifteen minutes, depending on your needs.

It can also be used as a guide for children storytellers. The skeleton is a flexible document and can be added to according to the person who uses it. There may be a phrase from the printed story that is not included in the skeleton that everyone wants to add. You can write that in. Make it the skeleton that will be the most helpful for you and your group of children. The process of choosing what is part of or omitted from the skeleton helps the children understand how the story works. You can create one-page skeletons for other stories you or the children might want to tell by writing the skeleton on a large paper or on a chalkboard.

The story skeleton offers the essential elements of a story to allow the tale to be more malleable for your own unique storytelling. There is a tendency to want to hide notes for telling a story, but hiding the story skeleton is a disservice to you and to the children with whom you work. You can explain to them what the skeleton is. If they cannot read, you can even add symbols, and they can use it to retell the tale themselves. Likewise early readers can be encouraged to use it and retell the tale. These activities help them understand story and to develop their own oral expression. The story skeleton can become an active element in your story world!

Picture Books

At the end of each chapter is a list of some excellent picture books that can further your exploration of the focus of the chapter. It is nice for children to have an illustrated book in hand that supports the work we have started. If you do not have one of the books listed, you likely have another that will work as well. At the close of the book is a reference list of folktale collections. These are great sources for you to discover additional stories to support further explorations of the themes in this book or for other areas of study.

Conclusion

Now that this introduction is coming to a close, it's time for you to use *Stories in Action*. Remember, however, that the stories are not in action unless *you* set them in motion. There are many suggestions in the book to help you activate these tales, but the single most important factor in this book's success is how you think of the tales. If you feel you must use the stories as they are presented, you may miss out on ideas that work better for you and the children with whom you work.

It certainly makes sense to begin with the way the stories and activities are presented. After all, years have gone into finding just the right stories and massaging the activities so that they work beautifully. Remember, though, that these very stories and activities continue to change from year to year and group to group. An activity that works grandly with one group of four-year-olds may need to be slowed down, sped up, or saved for another time with another group of the same age children. That is the challenge and joy of working with children. You never know, but you can watch, listen, and trust that these stories will serve you well if you use them with your knowledge of the children in front of you.

There are fifteen finger plays and twenty-seven additional stories in this book as well as language-rich activities. I have seen hundreds of children delight in these tales and activities. I hope that you find the work helpful and inspiring and experience the joy of watching a group of young children enthusiastically acting out a story as you tell it. May you also have the thrill of hearing a child proudly retell a tale or share a new creation. Here we go!

Part One

Exploring Themes through Stories

Chapter 1
Tales of Crowded Dwellings

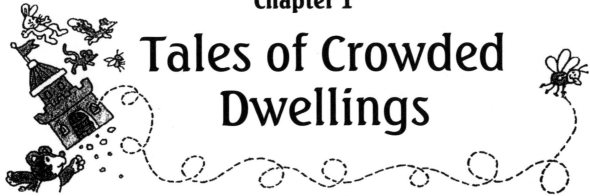

Although an unusual theme to begin a book, it is an idea shared by exciting children's stories from many lands. One of these stories is "The Fly's Castle," an old tale from Russia that takes place in a snowy forest. Here it is presented as a Finger Play to launch this exploration of *Stories in Action*. It is a wonderful story that will immediately engage the child participants. Following the Finger Play, the chapter offers other delightful stories and activities to ensure that you return to this book many times.

Finger Play Warm-Up

After the basic warm-up, you can begin the story. When you introduce the fly, create a fly with your hand as in the illustration below, then move it about to indicate "flying." Invite the child listeners to make a fly, too. They will copy your movement. Then the children will be ready to join in on the other finger play characters as you introduce them during the telling of the tale. By inviting the girls and boys to join the fly's flight, you make it clear that you want them to help you tell the story with their finger play.

The Fly's Castle

A Folktale from Russia

One day, a **fly** built her very own castle.

Along came a flea who asked,
"Who's in fly's castle?"

"I!" said the fly.
"Come on in!"
And the flea flew in.

Then **along came a mouse** who asked,
"Who's in Fly's castle?"

"I!" said the fly.
"And me!" called the flea.
"Come on in!"
And the mouse crawled in.

Then along came a hare who asked,
"Who's in Fly's castle?"

"I!" said the fly.
"And me!" called the flea.
"Me, too!" cried the mouse.
"Come on in!"
And the hare hopped in.

Then along came a fox who asked,
"Who's in Fly's castle?"

"I!" said the fly.
"And me!" called the flea.
"Me, too!" cried the mouse.
"Ya-hoo!" said the hare.
"Come on in!"
And the fox leapt in.

Then along came a wolf who asked,
"Who's in Fly's castle?"
"I!" said the fly.
"And me!" called the flea.
"Me, too!" cried the mouse.
"Ya-hoo," said the hare.
"I'm here," cried the fox.
"Come on in!"
And the wolf went in.

Then along came a bungling bear who asked, "Who's in Fly's castle?"

"I!" said the fly.
"And me!" called the flea.
"Me, too!" cried the mouse.
"Ya-hoo!" said the hare.
"I'm here," cried the fox.
"Hear! Hear!" wailed the wolf.
"Come on in!"

But that great big bungling bear,
Without even being aware,
with a swing of its paw
sent the castle and all
on a flight right up into the air!

The End

Storytelling Tips (All Ages)

Make a megaphone with your hands and call out through the megaphone, "Who's in Fly's Castle?" This further engages the children with an active way to be part of the story. They will make megaphones too and join in on the question, "Who's in Fly's Castle?" Repeat for all the characters that visit.

 LITERACY CONNECTION: The children enjoy hearing the simple rhymes of the animals and their responses. This helps build **phonological awareness** and **vocabulary**. They hear and soon they join in. Because it is a cumulative tale, the rhymes are repeated, so the children join in on the repetition and pick up on the new phrase.

Activity: Acting out the Story (Pre-K–Grade 1)

Background: This is really a great story to act out. Because of the bear's action at the end of the tale, for years I did not use this story for acting out. I thought someone might get hurt and I was sure that the one or two that are always knocking over blocks would wish to be the bear(s). However, one day, after telling *The Fly's Castle,* the children begged to act out the story. So we gave it a try. The children all became the animals, and sure enough, as expected, the kid who I thought would be the bear became the bear.

Then the magic happened. Standing up big and strong, the bear swung out into the air but he was far from the fly's castle where all the others were huddled. He played the bear, and he watched out for the rest of the class. The children who were "in the castle" went flying and called out joyfully—great fun was had by all. The child who normally knocks down blocks got to be that sort of character in a story, and it was all right. He didn't get in trouble. In fact, he was an important part of the story! And he watched out for the others. Since then, the children I work with always act out this story, and after dozens of times with many, many groups of children, it remains a safe and exuberant activity. Another interesting thing has occurred. It is not unusual for a child who would never knock anything down to choose to be the bear. It seems the story offers a safe place to explore feelings and actions by being part of a story.

The Action: Follow the "Acting Out Stories" suggestions in the introduction. After sharing the story, point out spots around the "acting out space" for the different characters: Fly, Flea, Mouse, Bunny (Rabbit for first graders), Fox, Wolf, and Bear. Ask if you left out any characters. Once in a while, someone wants to be the castle. When this occurs, it's fun to see how the children devise methods for the castle to contain all the characters. Then retell the story as the children act it out.

Tips for Expanding the Story: Depending on the time you wish to take on the activity, you can expand the story. The expansion allows for more movement and action. Some examples:

- As each character is added, describe how it moves through the snowy forest.

- When each character enters the castle, tell how the others offer the newcomer something to eat, like cheese for the mouse.

- After the character-filled castle has flown through the sky, describe how each animal scurries back home.

Additional Notes: When enacting this story, the children often say the lines of the characters. It is not unusual for a child to say the entire phrase, "I, said the fly," because that is how the story was heard. Sometimes the children feel shy and don't speak at all and then you just say the lines for their characters. They will want to act this story out more than once, and often saying the dialogue shifts to the children on the second, third, or fourth time. Repeating the story also allows the children to change characters. Of course, unless you have a very small group, you will have more than one of most of the characters. When no one chooses one of the characters, it provides a good opportunity to discuss the needs of the story and the importance of the various characters (even the pre-K can explore this). Generally one or more children will offer to be that character.

 LITERACY CONNECTION: Noticing the importance of the various characters in a story is a valuable tool for the prereader and for the early reader as well: they are learning how a story functions and increasing their **understanding of the narrative!**

Activity: Children Retelling the Tale (Grades 2–4)

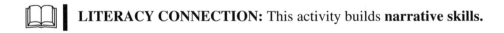 **LITERACY CONNECTION:** This activity builds **narrative skills.**

"The Fly's Castle" and many of the other finger plays in this book are great tales for the children to tell to others. The finger play and the repetition in the story help them remember its structure and make it a fun tale for young storytellers. If you plan on having the children telling the story to others, you should discuss strategies for remembering and telling. Here's a sample dialogue:

Bill: Let's talk about what's important when you're telling this story.

Children: Well, the fly has to build a castle.

Bill: That's true. Does a flea have to be the first visitor?

Children: No, but the animals get bigger.

Bill: Does each animal have to be bigger for the story to make sense?

Children: No, but it makes it easier to remember. [And so on.]

The children enjoy these explorations because they support their desire to be storytellers. In the meantime, they have looked at the story and discovered many important elements. This is useful for any encounter with a story in oral or written form.

Group Discussion: The Structure of the Tale (Grades 2–4)

"The Fly's Castle" is a cumulative tale. Cumulative tales are explored in Chapter 13. Here, it is good for the students to experience a cumulative story, tell it, and possibly act it out without going into its structural home base. If you use Chapter 13 later in the year, you can see who remembers this story, or you can tell it again in the midst of the other stories presented.

The next story originated with the game that follows it.

The Quiet Evening

I was going to have a quiet evening at home. I decided to take a nice warm bath. So I ran the water and just as the bath was full, I heard a knock on the door—KNOCK, KNOCK, KNOCK. I counted, "1, 2, 3" and called out, "Who is it?" but nobody answered, so I walked over to the door and opened it. In came a crocodile, who walked by me, into the bathroom, and slid into the tub! So much for the bath.

So I decided to just read a book. I picked up my book, turned on the lamp next to the couch, and just as I was sitting down I heard, KNOCK, KNOCK, KNOCK. I counted, "1, 2, 3" and called out, "Who is it?" but nobody answered, so I walked over to the door and opened it. A kangaroo hopped through the door and landed on the couch right on top of my book! So much for reading my book.

So I decided to get a snack, but just when I opened the refrigerator, I heard KNOCK, KNOCK, KNOCK. I counted, "1, 2, 3" and called out, "Who is it?" but nobody answered, so I walked over to the door and opened it. A tiger padded through the door and into the kitchen. The tiger climbed into my refrigerator and started eating! So much for a snack.

So I thought I'd just read a magazine. I started to sit down when KNOCK, KNOCK, KNOCK. I counted, "1, 2, 3" and called out, "Who is it?" but nobody answered, so I walked over to the door and opened it. A little bunny rabbit hopped in and hopped up onto the chair and started nibbling my magazine. So much for that magazine!

So there was a crocodile in my tub, a kangaroo on my book on the couch, a tiger eating my food, and a bunny rabbit nibbling on my magazine. I thought I'd just go to bed. I put on my pajamas and just as I spread back the covers I heard, KNOCK, KNOCK, KNOCK. I counted, "1, 2, 3" and called out, "Who is it?" but nobody answered, so I walked over to the door and opened it. In came … [Move to the following game.]

Activity: The Knock-Knock Game (Pre-K–Grade 1)

After you say the phrase, "In came …" in the preceding story, you explain this game that continues the narrative by having more animals enter the house.

Each child gets to knock on the "door" and be any animal she or he wishes. The "door" can be almost anything—a real door, a curtain, or just two chairs to make an entranceway. All the children should be on one side where there is room for the animal to move around; when finished, they go to a different side, where all the animals end up. After the guest has knocked, the other children join in with you and call out, "1, 2, 3! Who is it?" Depending on the age group and the number of times you've played, you can add the following ideas:

1. Have the child announce what animal she or he is and show that animal in the open space.

2. Let everyone guess what animal the child is pretending to be. Three guesses and then the performer says what the animal is. (If there is movement that suggests the animal, you can point it out while they are trying to guess. It offers movement vocabulary.)

3. Ask the animal to tell where in the house she or he is going.

The game continues until all the children have entered the house as animals. They can then all play or go to sleep. This ends the game and the story.

Activity: Children Adding to a Story (Grades 2–4)

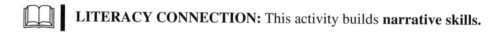 **LITERACY CONNECTION:** This activity builds **narrative skills.**

With children of this age, the Knock-Knock game just described can turn into an oral exercise rather than an acted-out one. After you tell "The Quiet Evening" up to the entrance of the children's animals, each can *tell* which animal enters the house, where it goes, and what it does. After all the animals have entered, the children can offer endings for the story.

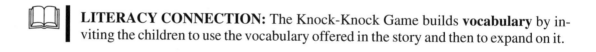 **LITERACY CONNECTION:** The Knock-Knock Game builds **vocabulary** by inviting the children to use the vocabulary offered in the story and then to expand on it.

The following old folktale continues the exploration of crowded places and sets up a great next-step activity after the children's participation in the Knock-Knock Game. It has been retold to set up the activities that follow.

The Farmer's Noisy House

A Tale from Poland

There once was a farmer who lived by himself. Oh, he had animals of course, but they lived in the barn or out in the pastures. The farmer had his home all to himself. Then one day he went to his mailbox and found a letter from his sister. He opened it and read these words: "Dear Brother, My children have spent all of their lives in the city with me. I would like them to live in the country for a change. I was wondering if my children could come and stay with you this summer. Your loving sister, Olga."

The farmer smiled and thought, "It gets a little lonesome on this farm. It'll be nice to have some children." So he wrote back to his sister that he would welcome the visit.

Summer came and the children arrived. There were six of them, three sisters and three brothers. They ran up to the farmer and asked, "Uncle Farmer, Uncle Farmer, what can we do?"

He looked at the children and asked, "Have you ever ridden a horse?"

The children shook their heads. "We've never ridden horses; we live in the city."

The farmer asked, "Would you like to?"

"Yes!" they exclaimed, and so the farmer showed them how to ride, and they galloped across the fields.

The next day, they came to their uncle again, "Uncle Farmer, Uncle Farmer, what can we do today?"

"Have you ever milked a cow?" he asked.

"Of course not, " the children responded, "We live in the city."

"Would you like to?" he asked.

"Sure," they exclaimed, and the farmer taught them how to milk a cow. They also learned to feed the ducks, slop the pigs, and shear the sheep. They learned to wake up with the rooster.

But then one day, they woke up and saw it was raining. It was raining really hard. They ran to their uncle in the kitchen, "Uncle Farmer, Uncle Farmer, what do we do today? It's raining."

The farmer shrugged his shoulders. "I don't know," he said.

"Oh," sighed the children.

The next day it was raining again. The children went into the kitchen, "Uncle Farmer, Uncle Farmer, what do we do today?"

"I don't know," replied the farmer.

"Oh," moaned the children.

Day after day it rained. The children had nothing to do! They ran to their uncle and asked, "Uncle Farmer, Uncle Farmer, do you have any puzzles?" The farmer shook his head, "I'm a farmer; I don't have puzzles."

"Ohhh," groaned the kids. They got another idea. "Uncle Farmer, Uncle Farmer, do you have any books for children?"

Once again the farmer shook his head. "I don't have children's books; I'm a farmer."

"Ohhh," groaned the children.

"Uncle Farmer, Uncle Farmer, do you have any markers and paper?"

The farmer shook his head, "I don't have markers or crayons or books or puzzles or games. I'm a farmer."

"Ohhhh," moaned and groaned the children.

Then they had an idea. They decided to sing and they made up a new song. It went like this:

Yi, Yi, Yi, Yi, Yi, Yi, Yi

Yi, Yi, Yi, Yi, Yi, Yi, Yi

They thought it was a funny song, and it made them laugh. And as they laughed and sang, they jumped up and down:

Yi, Yi, Yi, Yi, Yi, Yi, Yi

Yi, Yi, Yi, Yi, Yi, Yi, Yi

But they all STOPPED when they saw their uncle running out the door with his hands over his ears. The farmer ran through the rain up over the hill and into the village. He ran until he came to the wisewoman's house. He knocked on her door.

The wisewoman answered the door, "Yes? What's the problem?" she asked.

The farmer was panting from all that running, "The children! The children!" he said.

The wisewoman seemed surprised, "But you don't have any children."

"I know," he said, "It's the rain."

"The rain is a problem?" asked the wisewoman. "I thought you were a farmer. You should love the rain."

"I do," said the farmer, "But you see I have children staying with me and they can't go out because of the rain. Now all they do all day is jump up and down and sing,

Yi, Yi, Yi, Yi, Yi, Yi, Yi

Yi, Yi, Yi, Yi, Yi, Yi, Yi

The wisewoman listened and then she asked, "Do you have any cows?"

"Of course!" replied the farmer, "I'm a farmer.

"Well," she said, "Do you have any horses?"

"Of course!" replied the farmer, "I'm a farmer.

"Well," she said, "Do you have any ducks?"

"Of course!" replied the farmer, "I'm a farmer.

"Well then," said the wisewoman, "Take two cows and two horses and five little ducks, and bring them into your house."

"What?" asked the astonished farmer.

The wisewoman repeated, "Take two cows and two horses and five little ducks and bring them into your house."

"OK; you're the wise one," said the farmer and he set out through the rain back to his farmhouse. When he got there, he let two cows, two horses, and five little ducks into his house. The animals had never been in his house before, and so they all started making noise.

The cows mooed, "Mooooooo!"

The horses neighed, "Nei–igh!"

And the five little ducks started going, "Quack, quack, quack!"

When the children heard all this noise they thought it was so funny that they started jumping up and down again, singing their song: "Yi-Yi-Yi-Yi-Yi-Yi-Yi."

But they all STOPPED when they saw the farmer running out the door into the rain with his hands over his ears. He ran until he came to the wisewoman's door. He knocked and she answered, "Yes?"

The farmer was panting and said, "It's even noisier!"

"What do you mean?" asked the woman.

"Well, now," he replied,

"The Cows are mooing, 'Moooo!'

The horses are neighing, 'Neigh!'

The ducks are quacking, 'Quack, quack, quack!'

And the kids are still jumping up and down saying,

'Yi-Yi-Yi-Yi-Yi-Yi-Yi

Yi-Yi-Yi-Yi-Yi-Yi-Yi-Yi!'

The wisewoman listened and then she asked, "Do you have any pigs?"

"Of course!" replied the farmer, "I'm a farmer.

"Well," she said, "Do you have any sheep?"

"Of course!" replied the farmer, "I'm a farmer.

"Well," she said, "Do you have any chicks?"

"Of course!" replied the farmer, "I'm a farmer."

"Well then," said the wisewoman, "Take three pigs and three sheep and four little chicks and bring them into your house."

"What?" asked the astonished farmer.

The wisewoman repeated, "Take three pigs and three sheep and four little chicks and bring them into your house."

"OK, you're the wise one," said the farmer and he set out through the rain back to his farmhouse. When he got there he let three pigs, three sheep, and four little chicks into his house. The animals had never been in his house before, and so they all started making noise.

The pigs oinked, "Oink-Oink!"

The sheep baa-ed, "Baa-ah!"

And the four little chicks went, "Peep-Peep-Peep!"

When the children heard all this noise, they thought it was so funny and they started jumping up and down again, singing their song, "Yi-Yi-Yi-Yi-Yi-Yi-Yi!"

But they all STOPPED when they saw the farmer running out the door into the rain with his hands over his ears. He ran until he came to the wisewoman's door. He knocked and she answered, "Yes?"

The farmer was panting and said, "It's even noisier!"

"What do you mean?" asked the woman.

"Well, now," he replied,

"The pigs are oinking, "Oink, Oink!"

Sheep are baa-ing, 'Baa-ah!'

Chicks are peeping, 'peep-peep-peep!'

The Cows are still mooing, 'Moooooo!'

The horses are still neighing, 'Neigh!'

The ducks are still quacking, 'Quack, quack, quack!'

And the kids are still jumping up and down saying,

'Yi-Yi-Yi-Yi-Yi-Yi-Yi

Yi-Yi-Yi-Yi-Yi-Yi-Yi'

And it's driving me crazy!"

The wisewoman listened and then she asked, "Do you have any dogs?"

"Of course, but not in my house. They live outside!" replied the farmer.

"Well," she said, "Do you have any cats?"

"Of course!" replied the farmer, "I'm a farmer."

"Well," she said, "Do you have a rooster?"

"Of course!" replied the farmer, "I'm a farmer."

"Well then," said the wisewoman, "Take your dog and two cats and the rooster and bring them into your house."

"Are you kidding?" asked the astonished farmer.

The wisewoman repeated, "Take the dog and two cats and the rooster and bring them into your house."

"OK, you're the wise one," said the farmer and he set out through the rain back to his farmhouse. When he got there he let the dog, two cats, and the rooster into his house. The animals had never been in his house before, and so they all started making noise.

The dog barked "Ruff-ruff!"

The cats meowed, "Meow!"

And the rooster crowed, "Cock-a-doodle-do!"

When the children heard all this noise, they thought it was so funny that they started jumping up and down again, singing their song, "Yi-Yi-Yi-Yi-Yi-Yi-Yi!"

But they all STOPPED when they saw the farmer running out the door into the rain with his hands over his ears. He ran until he came to the wisewoman's door. He knocked and she answered, "Yes?"

The farmer was panting and said, "It's even noisier!"

"What do you mean?" asked the woman.

"Well, now," he replied,

"The dog is barking, 'Ruff-ruff!'

The cats are meowing, 'Meow!'

Rooster is crowing, 'Cock-a-doodle-do!'

Pigs are still oinking, 'Oink-oink-oink!'
Sheep are still baa-ing, 'Baa-ah!'
Chicks are still peeping, 'Peep-peep-peep!'
The cows are still mooing, 'Mooo!'
The horses are still neighing, 'Neigh!'
The ducks are still quacking, 'Quack, quack, quack!'
And the kids are still jumping up and down saying,
'Yi-Yi-Yi-Yi-Yi-Yi-Yi!
Yi-Yi-Yi-Yi-Yi-Yi-Yi!'
And it's driving me crazy!"
"Well," said the wisewoman. "Go back home and let all the animals go back outside."
"What?" whined the farmer.
The wisewoman repeated her advice. "Go back home and let all the animals go back outside."
"OK," said the farmer and trudged back home through the pouring rain. When he got there, he opened the door wide and let the cows go back into the pasture, and the horses ran out across the fields.
The ducks waddled out and went into the pond.
The pigs went and bathed in the mud.
The chicks went pecking for food on the ground.
The sheep wandered over the hill.
The dog and cats raced for the barn. That's where the rooster went as well.
The farmer went into his house. The kids were still jumping up and down singing their song,
"Yi-Yi-Yi-Yi-Yi-Yi-Yi!
Yi-Yi-Yi-Yi-Yi-Yi-Yi'!"
But now it didn't seem so loud to the farmer. In fact he kind of liked that little song! He started singing it with the children and jumping up and down!
But they all STOPPED! When one of the girls called out, "Look! It stopped raining."
They ran outside and went horseback riding for the rest of the day.

The End

Activity: Acting out the Story (Pre-K–Grade 1)

Although it does get a little noisy, this is a fabulous story for acting out. After sharing the story, name characters and point out positions around the "acting out space." Remember to ask if there's a character you missed. Sometimes children have favorite farm animals that did not get mentioned that can easily be included. Your attention to the children's response to the story enriches their experience and whets their appetite for more stories and activities. Once in a while, no one wants to be the wisewoman (or man) in town. In this circumstance, you can be the wise one. This is perhaps the only time you should take on a role in a story, because this character functions outside of the action.

Remind everyone of the three rules for acting out stories:

1. Listen to the storyteller.

2. Be safe!

3. Have fun!

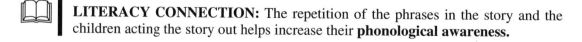 **LITERACY CONNECTION:** The repetition of the phrases in the story and the children acting the story out helps increase their **phonological awareness.**

Tips for Retelling the Story for the Activity. Use the skeleton (see below) for retelling the tale. Let your words sometimes initiate and sometimes follow the children's actions. If there are just a few "children" and many "animals," you may want to spend less time on the farm activities when the children first arrive. These are things you can adjust as you go. As you tell stories for acting out more often, you will gain clarity in how to time the different sections. Children absolutely love to act out stories, so if you give it a chance, you will have plenty of opportunities to hone your skills.

You will notice in the story that every time the farmer runs out the door, the noise and jumping stops. This was not how it was originally told. It was added so that instead of breaking the narrative of the story to tell the children to be quiet, the narrative itself has the children stopping their noise. The children readily accept this reality for it is what happens in the story! You can use this idea in many circumstances!

Tips for Using the Story Skeleton for the Activity: As described in the introduction, the story skeleton offers a flexible bare-bones outline of the story for your retelling. Flexibility is key in retelling a tale for acting out. After all, it is very likely that there will be two or three farmers instead of one and maybe the animals on the farm will be different from those named in the story. The skeleton makes this easy for you to do while still maintaining the integrity of the story.

Each time this story is acted out, it goes a little differently. Sometimes a child playing the farmer will remember and say all the lines of the farmer. Sometimes the child says nothing, and you say the lines for her. Just be ready to go with the children. As you do more and more stories you, and they, will gain confidence.

These acted-out stories can be turned into little plays that offer a wonderful first acting experience. It is a no-mistake model for performance. The script is built so that the narrator can always say the dialogue. Children do not need to memorize lines. If the character says the speech instead of or in addition to the narrator, it still works wonderfully.

The Skeleton for "The Farmer's Noisy House"

1. A farmer lives alone on his farm.

2. His six nieces and nephews come to stay for the summer.

3. They have fun.

4. It starts raining.

5. Children are bored.

6. They decide to sing and dance. It is noisy!

7. They STOP when they see the farmer running out of the house with his hands over his ears.

8. The farmer explains to the wisewoman about the noisy children.

9. She tells him to put some farm animals in the house.

10. He does. They make their sounds. Children sing. It's noisier!

11. The farmer runs back into town.

12. The wisewoman tells him to add more animals.

13. It's even noisier!

14. The whole cycle repeats.

15. Finally, the wisewoman says to let the animals out of his house.

16. He does.

17. The children's singing does not seem so loud.

18. He joins them in their singing.

The End

From *Stories in Action: Interactive Tales and Learning Activities to Promote Early Literacy* by Bill Gordh. Westport, CT: Libraries Unlimited. Copyright © 2006.

The stories and activities in this chapter can be repeated many times throughout the year with the children playing different parts. Each time you retell a story, it gives you the chance to make the process more organic.

The following picture books also explore the theme of the crowded habitat. It is fun to share illustrated books with the children and they begin to see how even today's authors are still using ideas from tales told long ago.

Thematic Picture Book Suggestions

 LITERACY CONNECTION: Print Motivation: After building excitement into the notion of crowded habitats, offering books that further explore the theme will make them enticing.

Donaldson, Julia, and Axel Scheffeler (illustrator). *Room on the Broom.* Dial Books for Young Readers, 2001.

Supraner, Robyn, and Irene Trevas (illustrator). *No Room for a Sneeze.* Troll Communications, 1986.

Tresselt, Alvin, and Yaroslova (illustrator). *The Mitten.* HarperTrophy, 1989.

Wood, Audrey, and Don Wood (illustrator). *The Napping House.* Red Wagon Books, 2000.

Chapter 2
Tales Using Echoes and Reflection

Repetition is often used in stories with young children. Repetition and rhythm are two elements that fortify young readers (or prereaders) as they make their way through a story. Echoes are thematic kin to repetition and can be used in storytelling to invite the participation of the listener. Call-and-Response (which could be called "Call and Echo") is an African-based form used in song and story and sometimes movement games. It provides a meaningful relationship between leader and follower. The stories in this chapter involve echo as an element. The teller can seize this element and use it to include listeners by asking them to "be the echo." As is the habit of this book, I start this chapter with a finger play. In a way, every finger play is an echo story because the children are constantly echoing the movement of your fingers. In this finger play, there is a specific vocal echo in the middle of the tale.

Finger Play Warm-Up

Now the children are ready to help accompany the story.

The Six Silly Cats in Calico Caps

Based on a Folktale from France

Once long ago, there were six cats—three brother cats and three sister cats. Let's count them!

One cat,

Two cats,

Three cats,

Four cats,

Five cats,

Six cats!

Everyone called them the six silly cats in calico caps because it seemed like something funny was always happening to them, and they always wore calico caps.

One day they decided to take a long walk together. The six cats put on their six calico caps and started **walking.** The cats had rarely been out of the village and they saw a lot of amazing sights.

When they came to a well, the six silly cats were not sure what it was. They moved carefully to the well's edge. Then they **looked deep down inside.** "Meow!" they called.
"Meow!" the well echoed back.

The echo scared the six silly cats and **they went running!**

When they finally slowed down, one of the sisters was worried. She said, **"That meow from the well sounded just like us. Maybe one of us fell in!"**

The oldest brother scratched his head. He said, "Look, I'll count us and then we'll know if all six of us are here."

The oldest brother started counting:

One cat,

Two cats,

Three cats,

Four cats,

Five cats!

He counted again:

One cat,

Two cats,

Three cats,

Four cats,

Five cats!

He counted again!

One cat,

Two cats,

Three cats,

Four cats,

Five cats!

Only five! You see, he forgot to count himself. He looked at his sister. "You're right," he said, "there are only five of us here. One of us must have fallen in!"

All six cats went running back to the well.

The oldest brother looked down into the well. He saw his reflection in the water. He turned to the others and said, "I see one of us down there. Give me a hand!"

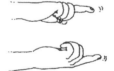

 So, hanging on to one another, they lowered the oldest brother down into the well. Just as they were getting close to the bottom, the sister holding the oldest brother called out, "We're almost there!"

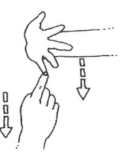

The four other cats got so excited they started clapping and cheering. **Then all six cats in their calico caps went tumbling down into the well.**

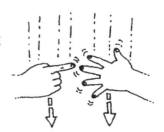

They were all tangled up in that well for a while. And all six cats got their calico caps soaking wet. Then they threw the caps up out of the well and **climbed out themselves.**

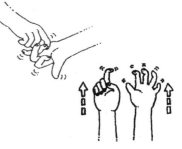

Once they were all back on the grass, the oldest saw the caps on the ground, **and counted them:**

One cap,

Two caps,

Three caps,

Four caps,

Five caps,

Six caps!

The oldest brother announced, "It was lucky we came back, because as you can see, we now have our six calico caps which means we are all back together."

They put on their caps and **the six silly cats in calico caps walked on,** whistling a happy tune!

The End

Storytelling Tips (All Ages)

Although not crucial to the meaning of the story, here are a few additions that make it more fun for the listeners. When the telling of the story is fun, boys and girls tend to become more involved.

1. Rather than introducing the six calico caps at the beginning, have the cats wander around the village without their caps for a while, meowing as they walk. "Meow, Meow, Meow-meow-meow. Meow, Meow, Meow-meow-meow." Children love joining in on the meow song and moving their six fingers as the cats stroll through town.

2. As the cats meow, mention that many people love their song, but some people don't. The ones who don't open their shutters and call out, "Quiet you cats!" The cats tiptoe by and then start singing again. Go through this little sequence a few times. This gets everyone animatedly involved in the story.

3. Then tell how the cats decide to leave the village and put on their "Adventure Calico Caps." Then count the caps together, "One cap, two caps…."

4. When the cats get to the well, discuss what a well is and what happens if you call into a well. [It echoes.] Then ask the children if they will be the echo. They always say, "Yes."

5. After the cat has sounded the alarm that one of them is missing, the brother counts. Count the finger cats so that one or more of the children notice and call it out before you tell what happened. This gives them a sense of "owning the story."

6. When the cats return to the well, have the oldest cat tell the others to stand back, and move your one hand with the five cats away. Then bring back your hand with one finger extended to show the reflection. This will make that idea clearer.

These ideas are not necessary for a successful story. The finger play as presented earlier works beautifully, but these are little things that can make it even more compelling. You should continue to notice how your children respond to the story and make your own adjustments.

Activity: Children Retelling the Tale (Grades 3 and 4)

 **LITERACY CONNECTION:** This activity builds **narrative skills.**

Third and fourth graders can tell "The Six Silly Cats" story at home to family or to other classes. They can tell it individually or as a group of storytellers with all the children leading the finger play.

Now we leave the village in France and move east to Macedonia for an amusing tale that also uses a well and its reflective capacity.

The Moon in the Well

A Tale from Macedonia

The full moon was high in the sky when Magda went to the well in the middle of the village to get a bucket of water. She was just about to drop the bucket in the well when she saw the reflection of the moon in the water at the bottom of it. Magda panicked. "The moon fell into the well!" she cried and ran to the nearest neighbor's house.

She knocked on the neighbor's door, and when he opened the door, Magda cried,

Help, help

Help, help

The moon has fallen

Into the well!

The neighbor, Jon, looked at Magda and exclaimed, "Let's tell everyone!" and together they ran to the next house and knocked. When the door opened, they cried,

Help, help

Help, help

The moon has fallen

Into the well!

Now there were three heading to the next house and rapping on the door.

Help, help

Help, help

The moon has fallen

Into the well!

Husband and wife joined them this time and now there were five running to the next house and knocking,

Help, help

Help, help

The moon has fallen

Into the well!

The whole family—father, mother, grandmother, and four children—joined the party of announcers and on they traveled. At each house the call was the same:

Help, help

Help, help

The moon has fallen

Into the well!

The whole village ran to the well. A few at a time peered into the well, and they all saw the same thing. There was the moon down in the bottom of the well. They looked at each other. Jon had an idea: "I'll go home and get a rope and a big hook and together we can pull the moon out and save it!"

"Hooray," cried the others as Jon ran home to get the rope and hook.

When he returned they threw the hook end of the rope into the well. It so happened that the hook caught on a rock in the wall of the well. So when everyone grabbed the rope and pulled, nothing happened except the rope pulled tight. Everyone called out, "Pull harder!" And they did! They pulled! They pulled and pulled and pulled and pulled and—the hook slipped off the rock and came flying out. All the pullers fell on their backs on the ground.

Lying on the ground, the villagers looked into the nighttime sky, and what did they see? The full moon! The villagers smiled. Then they cheered and starting shouting, "We did it! We did it! We saved the moon!"

The villagers were so proud of themselves. In fact if you wander into that little village in Macedonia, they will probably tell you about the night they saved the moon!

The End

Storytelling Tips (All Ages)

The little refrain the woman uses to alert the neighbors is not necessary for the meaning of the story. However, it offers the children a chance to join in on the repeated lines.

 LITERACY CONNECTION: Creating the circumstance for the children to be active participants in the telling of a tale makes them more eager listeners and helps them **understand the narrative.** The refrain in the story uses a partial rhyme that builds **phonological awareness.**

The Skeleton for "The Moon in the Well"

1. A woman goes to get water from the village well at night.

2. The full moon is in the sky.

3. The woman sees the moon's reflection in the well water.

4. The woman thinks the moon fell into the well.

5. The woman runs and tells all the neighbors.

6. The neighbors all run to well and see moon.

7. The neighbors get rope with a hook and throw it into well to save moon.

8. The hook catches on a rock.

9. Everyone pulls on the rope.

10. The hook comes loose; everyone falls down.

11. Lying on the ground, they look up at full moon.

12. They cheer!

13. They are sure they saved the moon.

The End

This chapter started in France with "The Six Silly Cats." From there we traveled east to Macedonia, just above Greece. For the third story, we continue east and share a story from India that also uses the reflective and echoing aspects of a well. The story is a bit more complicated, and the telling incorporates the fact that the children have already participated in the telling of "The Six Silly Cats." As a result, your listeners are ready to be the echo in the well.

The Lion in the Well

A Tale from India

All the animals in the jungle called it the "Lion's Jungle." The reason was that the lion had all the animals terrified. He was so strong and so quiet and always hungry. Lion wandered through the jungle on his padded paws as quiet as can be. Out of the corner of his eye, he would spot a squirrel coming down the tree. Before the squirrel even saw the lion, it found itself swooped away and swallowed! The lion was always hungry and in "his" jungle, he was King!

Well all the other animals were frightened all the time. They never knew when the lion might quietly, sneakily come through the jungle and eat one of them for lunch. The animals had to do something. So they called a meeting. All the animals gathered—all the animals except the lion, that is. They looked at their friend Turtle, who often had good ideas. Turtle thought and thought and came up with a suggestion. She said, "Why don't we offer the lion an animal for lunch every day if he will stop hunting us? Then we won't be scared all the time." The other animals thought it was a great idea, so they all went together to see Lion.

When Lion saw them, he was excited and ready to gobble up everyone right then and there. But the other animals calmed him down and explained that they had come with a proposal. They explained their idea. Lion listened. "You mean," he said, "that everyday you will bring me one animal for lunch and I don't have to do a thing?" The other animals nodded. "And," continued Lion, "My lunch will always arrive exactly at noon?" The animals nodded again. Lion smiled, "I like this idea. I can just relax and my lunch comes to me!"

All the other animals thanked Lion and rushed off to have a celebration. The dancing and singing continued through the night. The next morning, the animals gathered. It was time to decide who would go get eaten by the lion. Squirrel shook his head, "No, I don't really want to go today. Maybe Deer would like to go!" Deer shook her head, "No, I don't really want to go today. Maybe turtle!" Turtle shook her head, "No, today's not a good day for me." This went on and on and on. None of the animals wanted to volunteer to get eaten by Lion. They all looked at Turtle for a solution.

Turtle had an idea, "Why don't we draw straws? We'll put the straws in a bundle so you can't tell which is which. Whoever picks the one long straw has to get eaten by Lion. That's fair." All the animals agreed. They gathered some straws with one very long straw and took turns picking. Squirrel chose a straw—a little tiny straw! Squirrel mopped his brow, "Scwoo!" and scampered up a tree. Turtle picked a straw—a little tiny straw, mopped her brow, "Scwoo!" Deer picked a straw—a little tiny straw, mopped her brow, "Scwoo!" Rabbit picked a straw—a long, long, long, long, long, long straw. "Oh no!" cried Rabbit, "I don't want to go!" But someone had to go, or they would be right back where they started. So Rabbit set off toward Lion's house.

Rabbit was clever and soon came up with a plan. Rabbit slowed her hop way down. By the time she got to Lion's, she was fifteen minutes late and Lion was angry. Rabbit spoke quickly, "Sorry I'm late! I'll jump right in your pot, but that other lion kind of threw me off." Lion looked up.

"Other lion? There are no other lions in MY jungle!" Lion roared.

Rabbit nodded and said, "That's what I thought. That's why I got confused. And this other lion looked ferocious, just like you!"

Lion nodded and smiled, "That's right. I'm ferocious."

"I know," continued Rabbit, "That's why I got mixed up. This other lion looked really mean, just like you."

"That's right," smiled Lion, "I am really mean."

"I know," said Rabbit, "That's why I got mixed up. At first I thought it was you, but now I'm here ready to jump in your pot!"

"Wait a minute!" roared Lion, "Can you show me where this other lion lives?"

"Yes," answered Rabbit, "But don't you want to eat me?"

"I'll eat you later, Rabbit. First I want to see this other lion."

"Follow me," said Rabbit and Lion followed Rabbit through the jungle. They traveled until they came to a well. Rabbit jumped up onto the wall of the well and pointed down into it. "The other lion is down there!" announced Rabbit who then hopped back onto the ground.

Lion bounded up onto the well wall and looked into the well. And what did he see? Right—his reflection—and Lion thought it was another lion. And when you call into a well, what do you hear? Right, an echo. Now you listeners be the echo, OK?

> **Lion:** Who are you?
>
> **Echo:** Who are you?
>
> **Lion:** I am Lion!
>
> **Echo:** I am Lion!
>
> **Lion:** This is my jungle!
>
> **Echo:** This is my jungle!
>
> **Lion:** No, it's my jungle.
>
> **Echo:** No, it's my jungle.
>
> **Lion:** My jungle!
>
> **Echo:** My jungle!
>
> **Lion:** I am ferocious!
>
> **Echo:** I am ferocious!
>
> **Lion:** I can roar louder!
>
> **Echo:** I can roar louder!
>
> **Lion:** I can!
>
> **Echo:** I can!
>
> **Lion:** Roar!
>
> **Echo:** Roar!
>
> **Lion:** ROAR!
>
> **Echo:** ROAR!
>
> **Lion:** ROAR!!!!!
>
> **Echo:** ROAR!!!!!

And with that the lion called out, "I'll get you!" and dove into the well. Rabbit jumped up on the well wall and waved good-bye to Lion, "Bye-bye!" Then she hopped back to her animal friends who were quite surprised to see her. Rabbit smiled and dusted off her front paws, "The lion problem has been taken care of!"

The End

The story "The Lion in the Well" is the activity and the invitation to join in is in the text itself. Following is the story's skeleton for your use when you retell the tale.

 LITERACY CONNECTION: By participating as the echo in the story children increase their **phonological awareness.**

The Skeleton for "The Lion in the Well"

1. Jungle animals are afraid of a ferocious lion.

2. Lion is always hunting the animals.

3. The animals have a meeting.

4. The animals decide to offer one animal a day to Lion if Lion will stop hunting.

5. They go to Lion and make the offer.

6. Lion accepts the offer. He says food must arrive at noon.

7. The animals leave happily. They have a party.

8. The next day, the animals must decide who will get eaten.

9. No one wants to go.

10. They draw straws—the one who draws the long straw will go to Lion.

11. Rabbit picks the long straw.

12. Rabbit has to go. She starts. She gets an idea. She slows down.

13. Rabbit is late; Lion is mad!

14. Rabbit tells Lion she saw another lion and thought it was him.

15. Lion says there are no other lions in *his* jungle!

16. Lion wants to see this other lion.

17. Rabbit leads him to a well in the jungle.

18. Lion leaps up onto well and sees his reflection in the water in the well.

19. Lion yells at his reflection. Echo.

20. Lion jumps into well to attack the other lion.

21. Rabbit returns to surprised friends.

From *Stories in Action: Interactive Tales and Learning Activities to Promote Early Literacy* by Bill Gordh. Westport, CT: Libraries Unlimited. Copyright © 2006.

These three stories provide a wonderful experience with the concept of echoes and reflections that can be extended into science. Here are some picture books that use echoes or reflection.

Thematic Picture Book Suggestions

 LITERACY CONNECTION: Print motivation. After building interest in the concept of echoes and reflection, offering books that further explore the theme motivates children to enjoy print stories.

Asch, Frank. *Happy Birthday Moon.* Aladdin Books, 2000 (rev. ed.).

Bahrampour, Ali. *Otto: The Story of a Mirror.* Farrar, Straus & Giroux, 2003.

Barnwell, Ysaye M., and Synthia Saint James. *No Mirrors in My Nana's House.* Harcourt Children's Books, 1998.

Henkes, Kevin. *Kitten's First Full Moon.* Greenwillow Press, 2004.

Kellogg, Stephen. *The Three Sillies.* Candlewick, 2004 (reprint ed.).

Pinkney, Brian. *Max Found Two Sticks.* Aladdin, 1997 (reprint ed.).

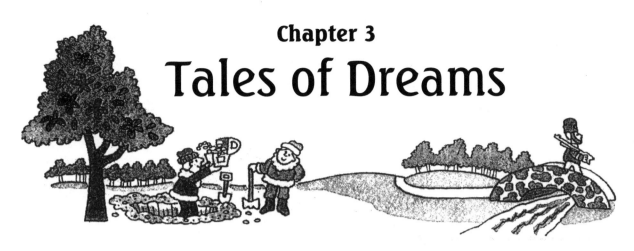

Chapter 3
Tales of Dreams

Dreams offer a wondrous, imaginative area for exploration. As the nature of dreams continues to be a mystery to scientists, we can use that mystery to make our own adventures even more exciting. Dreams, dream stories, and dream dances appear in every culture, and the tradition of Dreamtime is critical to the aboriginal people of Australia. We begin our dream adventures with a tale from Eastern Europe. There are many variations of this story told throughout Europe and England, and a similar tale is told in Japan as well.

Finger Play Warm-Up

In this story, the fingers do not represent characters in the tale. The gestures support the visualization of the story.

The Woodcutters

A Folktale from Poland

There was once a group of woodcutters who
lived together in a house on the edge of the woods.

It was a wooden house with a porch and a green roof.
Behind the house stood a **huge oak tree.**

One night the woodcutters had a dream.
In the dream **they walked** along a dirt road.
The road went up over a hill, down the other side
and **across a bridge.**

On the bridge stood **a guard wearing a red uniform with gold buttons and a tall black hat** with a golden eagle on its front.

In the dream, the woodcutters went under the bridge and **dug in the ground**. They dug until their shovels hit something hard. It was a chest. **They opened the lid.** It was filled with gold!

As soon as they saw the gold, they woke up. One of the woodcutters described the dream. The others exclaimed, **"Hey, we had that dream too!"**

But soon they forgot about the dream, and went into the forest to do their woodcutting. At the end of the day, they came home, ate their dinner and went to bed.

That night they all had the same dream!
—**walking down the road**—
—**coming to the bridge**—
—**the guard in the red uniform with the gold buttons and the tall black hat** with an eagle on its front—
—**digging under the bridge**—
—**opening the chest full of gold**—

They woke up.

"I had the same dream again!"
"Me, too!"
"Me, too!"
"Me, too!" chimed in the others.

But then they forgot about the dream, and went into
the forest to do their woodcutting.

At the end of the day, they came home, ate their
dinner, and went to bed.

That night they had the same dream
a third time!
—**walking down the road**—
—**coming to the bridge**—
—**the guard in the red uniform with the gold buttons and the tall black hat**
with an eagle on its front—
—**digging under the bridge**—
—**opening the chest full of gold**—

They woke up.
"I had the same dream again!"
"**Me, too!**"
"**Me, too!**"
"**Me, too!**" chimed in the others.

But this time they did not go to work. They decided
to follow their dream.

They walked and walked. They asked everyone
they met, " 'Do you know of a bridge with a guard in
a red uniform?" **People just shook their heads.** No
one had ever heard of such a place.

The woodcutters were about to give up when a traveler said he had seen the bridge and the guard in the red uniform. He gave them directions.

They walked and walked 'til they thought they would drop. The woodcutters came up over a hill and below them **they saw the bridge!** On the bridge stood **a guard in a red uniform with gold buttons and a tall black hat** with a golden eagle on its front.

They ran down the hill, and started under the bridge. The guard cried, "Halt! What are you doing?"

The woodcutters told the guard about their dream and their journey to his bridge.

The guard laughed, "You came all the way here because of a silly dream!? Well, this is the King's bridge and the King's land and you cannot dig here. So you may as well go back home."

Then the guard added, "You certainly have wasted your time. I had the same dream **three times,** but I certainly did not leave my post at the bridge to follow that dream!"

One of the woodcutters asked, "What was your dream?"

The guard answered, "Oh, it was silly. I dreamed I came to a wooden house on the edge of the woods. I walked past the porch and behind the house, where **I dug** under a **big oak tree**. There I found **a treasure chest full of gold.** It was a wonderful dream, but I stayed right here. And you'd better get back to your woodcutting!"

The tired and disappointed woodcutters **began their long walk home.** All at once they stopped and looked at one another. Then, without a word, they started running for their home.

When they got there they ran around behind the house, and **started digging** under **the great oak tree.**

It wasn't long before the shovels hit something hard. **It was a treasure chest!** And it was full of gold!

The End

 LITERACY CONNECTION: The repeated report of the dream solidifies the understanding of the descriptive **vocabulary** for the young listener, building **narrative understanding** as well.

Activity: Acting out the Story (Pre-K–Grade 1)

This is a fun tale for this activity because the children get to act out both the story and the dream within the story. Acting out a dream provides a chance to use different ways of moving to suggest the different reality of the dream. As always, name the characters and assign places for each character around the "acting out" space. Then ask if there are other characters you have not named. For this tale, children often name the chest of gold as a character. Remind everyone of the rules: Listen to the storyteller! Be safe! and Have fun! Here are a few additional thoughts that are specific to this story to make the activity more successful.

1. Take a moment to discuss the "staging." You might want to go ahead and select places for the sleeping woodcutters and the bridge.

2. Describe the woodcutters' wake-up time and their preparation for the day—washing their faces, brushing their teeth, eating breakfast, and so on. It makes the acting out both more fun and the experience more real because it reflects the children's own experience.

3. When the woodcutters decide to skip work and follow their dream, have a child be the person whom they meet on the road. If no one has chosen that character, you can get one of the guards to play this role, too. If several volunteer, describe how the woodcutters ask as many travelers as you have. These are additions you can incorporate as you go. The fluidity of the exchange and how the story can expand allows the children to experience how a story can gain details.

Activity: Sharing Dream Stories (Grades 2–4)

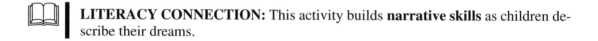

LITERACY CONNECTION: This activity builds **narrative skills** as children describe their dreams.

A story of a dream coming true (even in such a round-about way as this!) energizes the students' minds and imaginations about their own dreams. Ask your group who has had a dream that came true. Ask her/him to tell about the dream and what happened. Let other children share their dream stories. Have everyone write down their stories and illustrate them. Then collect those tales. You might make a book of them. If one of the children does not have a dream story to share, ask if she has ever had a dream she wished had come true. Usually you will see her eyes light up. Encourage her to write that dream story!

Activity: Creating Group Dream Stories (Grades 2–4)

LITERACY CONNECTION: This activity builds **narrative skills** as children listen to each other and build a story.

Because of the ability of a dream story to take unexpected turns, creating dream stories as a "going around the circle" story is also great fun. Have one child start the dream with a simple sentence or two and then say, "And then." The next child takes it from there. Each child adds just a little bit to the story and then says, "And then …" to pass it to the next teller. It's a good idea to let the story starter also finish the story, because then she or he can undo anything that made the child uncomfortable during the creation of the story. The story starter can give the story a title before beginning the tale or name it after the story is over. It is important for you not to make the titling decision, because letting the children choose makes them aware of how titles affect the tales. It is also fun to discuss how it affects the story with either choice.

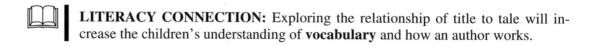

LITERACY CONNECTION: Exploring the relationship of title to tale will increase the children's understanding of **vocabulary** and how an author works.

Dreams figure in so many folktales that it was hard to know which ones to present in this book, but the determining factors are great stories that can lead to exciting and meaningful activities for the children. This next tale, traditionally told by the Pueblos of the American Southwest, is about the great trickster Coyote. As is often the case in trickster tales, the trickster gets tricked.

Coyote and the Meat

A Tale from the Pueblo American Indians

One day Coyote was walking down the road and doing what he often does. He was looking for food. Well, he hadn't walked far when he saw his friend Porcupine who called out, "What are you doing Coyote?" And Coyote replied, "Not very much. I'm just

Walking down the road

Walking down the road

Just looking for food

Looking for food."

Porcupine asked, "Can I join you?" and Coyote replied, "Sure!" So Porcupine joined Coyote, and together they went

Walking down the road

Walking down the road

Just looking for food

Looking for food.

They walked 'til they saw their friend Prairie Dog. Prairie Dog called out, "Hey Coyote, hey Porcupine, what are you doing?" And Coyote and Porcupine answered, "We're just

Walking down the road

Walking down the road

Just looking for food

Looking for food."

Prairie Dog asked, "Could I join you?" and the two friends said, "Sure!" So Prairie Dog joined them and now they were

Walking down the road

Walking down the road

Just looking for food

Looking for food.

They heard a bumpity-bumpity sound. It was a wagon coming their way! They jumped off the road just in time as the wagon bumpity-bumped its way by, leaving behind a cloud of dust. Coyote and Porcupine and Prairie Dog climbed back onto the road and watched the wagon. The back wheel of the wagon rolled over a big rock. The jolt sent a big piece of meat flying into the air and "Plop!" onto the ground.

Coyote, Prairie Dog, and Porcupine all saw the meat and cried out, "Food!" They ran down the road, and all three friends got to the meat at the same time. Porcupine announced, "This is great luck. Now we can share this meat and we will all have a good meal." "Great idea!" agreed Prairie Dog. But

Coyote did NOT want to share the meat and cried out, "No fair! No fair! No fair!" Prairie Dog and Porcupine stared at Coyote and asked, "What do you mean 'No fair'?" "Coyote announced, "I should get all the meat! I saw it first." "No you didn't," ventured Prairie Dog, "We all saw it at the same time." "And anyway," added Porcupine, "that doesn't matter, we should all share this good luck!"

But Coyote was not about to share the meat if he could help it. "OK, OK," said Coyote, "I don't want to have an argument. Let's just start all over again. I know! Let's have a race down that hill over there. The one who wins the race gets all the meat."

Prairie Dog and Porcupine knew there was no reason to try and argue with Coyote. "OK," they said and they started up the hill. Coyote followed, smiling. He looked at the short legs of his friends and at his nice long legs. Soon he would have all the meat for himself. They got to the top of the hill and asked a crow to caw and start the race.

"Caw! Caw! Caw!" and off they went! Coyote was laughing as he loped down the hill, but something came zipping by. What was that? When Coyote arrived at the bottom of the hill, Porcupine was already there! "I guess I get all the meat!" exclaimed Porcupine. Prairie Dog arrived, "That was a great idea, Porcupine! You get all the meat! You can really roll!"

"Roll!?!" screamed Coyote, "You don't win! You rolled! This was a running race!"

Porcupine shook her head. "You never said that. You just said it was a race. You're the one who didn't want to share the meat."

Coyote shouted, "No fair! No fair!"

Then Coyote got another idea. He smiled. "Wait a minute my friends, we don't need to have an argument. I've got a better idea. Here, we'll put the meat up in that tree where it will be safe. Now we all go to sleep. When we wake up, we'll tell our dreams. Whoever has the best dream will get all the meat. Now let's not argue. Just lie down and go to sleep."

Porcupine and Prairie Dog knew there was no reason to say anything, so they lay down under the tree. Soon Coyote was snoring and Prairie Dog was snoring and Porcupine was pretending to snore.

After a while Coyote woke up and yawned and called out, "Wake up, wake up!" Prairie Dog woke up and Porcupine pretended to wake up. They sat up, and Coyote wanted to go first. Now you might think this is a fair contest, but you should know that Coyote was known as a great dream teller, so it wasn't fair at all. Coyote told an amazing dream that completely entranced his two friends. After that, Prairie Dog told his dream. Coyote smiled. No one in the world would say Prairie Dog's dream was better. Now it was Porcupine's turn but Porcupine did not want to tell her dream.

"Come on," said Coyote, "We all must tell our dreams."

"All right," said Porcupine, "but it was not a great dream."

"Tell it!" ordered Coyote.

"Well," said Porcupine, "I dreamed I ate the meat."

"What?" asked Coyote.

"I dreamed I ate the meat," said Porcupine. Coyote stared at Porcupine. Then Coyote looked up into the tree. The meat was gone!

The End

Storytelling Tips (All Ages)

For the "walking down the road" refrain, use a "clap, then slap the thighs" to accompany yourself rhythmically. The students (even second and third graders) will join with you, and the movement will help them (and you) remember the words of the refrain.

Activity: Acting out the Story (Pre-K–Grade 1)

Name the characters and have the children stand in position around the space. Ask if there are additional characters. In this tale, a child might pick the wagon or the meat. (It is good not to name every character you can think of. The children stay more involved, knowing that you are open to their suggestions.) Recall the rules together: Listen to the Storyteller! Be safe! And have fun! Then retell the tale as they act it out. Use the skeleton if it is helpful. Here are a few specific points for this story.

- There will likely be many of all the animals, but if everyone wants to be porcupine, the story will not work. You can talk about this if it happens, and someone always comes to the rescue.

- Before starting, discuss and devise safe ways to go after the meat and to race down the hill. Having the group do this problem solving actively engages the children in the process of the activity. You might even move part of the story outside!

- When you reach the dream telling, you will find that some children recount what you told as the animal's dreams and others are ready to make up their own. Ask each child, "And what is your Prairie Dog (or Coyote) Dream?" Even if the children recount the same dream, it is a unique experience for each of them. When it comes to Porcupine, each porcupine will relish his or her own turn to say, "I dreamed I ate the meat!"

Activity: Creating Animal Dream Stories (All Ages)

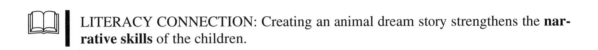 LITERACY CONNECTION: Creating an animal dream story strengthens the **narrative skills** of the children.

Setting Up the Activity: For this activity you may want to tell "Coyote and the Meat" a bit differently to offer some examples of dream stories. The story, as printed, just mentions that Coyote told an amazing dream. If you want to model a dream story for the children, you should have Coyote actually tell a dream at that point in the story. In case you feel at a loss creating a dream story for Coyote to tell, here's a possibility:

Coyote's Dream: "In my dream, Creator had decided that the nighttime sky was too dark, so Creator asked me, the great Coyote, to put the stars in the sky. I gathered little white flowers from the meadows and put them in a sack. When it got dark, I climbed into the sky and placed them there for everyone to see." (This Coyote Dream Story actually combines a number of Coyote and star stories in which Coyote is often not so heroic, although he would never admit it! Generally, he has messed up either by spilling the stars or by staying in the sky too long. When he tells the story himself, it changes.)

When it's Prairie Dog's turn, let Prairie Dog recount a short dream. This does two things: it gives the children a second model and it lets them know that it is fine to recount a short dream.

Prairie Dog's Dream: "In my dream, I was going through my tunnel and I crawled and I crawled and crawled. Finally I came out and I was on the moon!"

Guiding the Activity: Have the children choose an animal (not just ones from the story), lie down, and pretend to go to sleep. Older children can just sit in the circle and close their eyes. Tell everyone to let his or her animal fall asleep and dream. When their dream is over, they should sit up and form a circle. Then go around the circle letting all the children say what animal they are and then tell their animals' dream story. You may want to write these down as they are told. With older children, after telling their stories, they can write and illustrate their own dream tales. You can compile the stories in an animal dream book. If you are supporting a study of American Indian cultures, you can further the exploration by talking of the Native American notion of spirit animals in which each person has her or his own special animal. Many children chose an animal they feel that way about even without a discussion.

If you decide to do both the acting out and the animal dream activities, they should be done in different sessions.

The Skeleton for "Coyote and the Meat"

1. Coyote walks down the road, looking for food.

2. Coyote meets Porcupine.

3. Now it's Coyote and Porcupine walking down the road, looking for food.

   They meet Prairie Dog.

4. Now it's Coyote and Porcupine and Prairie Dog walking down the road, looking for food.

5. A wagon comes rumbling by.

6. They watch the wagon as it bumps over a rock.

   Meat flies out of the wagon and "plops!" on the road.

7. Three friends see the meat and run for it.

8. Porcupine and Prairie Dog want to share the meat.

9. Coyote wants the meat and claims he deserves it—"No Fair!"

10. Coyote suggests a race down the hill to determine who gets the meat.

11. Coyote has the longest legs.

12. They race.

13. Porcupine rolls down the hill and wins.

14. Coyote says, "No Fair!"

15. Coyote suggests putting the meat in a tree and that they all fall asleep.

16. They will share their dreams, and the best dream gets the meat.

17. They go to sleep. Porcupine pretends to be asleep.

18. Coyote tells dream.

19. Prairie Dog tells dream.

20. Porcupine says, "I dreamed I ate the meat!"

21. Coyote looks in tree.

22. The meat is gone!

23. Coyote can howl, "Ow-ooooooooo!"

The End

Dreams can be explored in many ways, and you can use these two stories to begin an exploration. The notion of "following your dream" is taken literally in the first story, and as often happens when one really follows a dream, the path does not lead where one expects. This story encourages the sharing of real dreams and dreams of what one hopes for. The dreams of hope offer another fertile subject area for the creation of stories and pictures. (See the picture book suggestions that follow.) The coyote dream story sets up the imaginative exploration of animal dreams. You can further enrich a dream study by exploring them in other art forms—painting, music, and dance, as well as literature.

Thematic Picture Book Suggestions

 LITERACY CONNECTION: Print motivation: after you engage children in the excitement of dreams, they will greet books that further the exploration with enthusiasm.

Heyer, Marilee. *The Weaving of a Dream: A Chinese Folktale.* Puffin Books, 1989.

Johnson, Angela, and Loren Long. *I Dream of Trains.* Simon & Schuster Children's Publishing, 2003.

King, Martin Luther Jr., and Kathleen A. Wilson (illustrator). *I Have a Dream.* Scholastic, 1997.

Osofsky, Audrey, and Ed Young (illustrator). *Dreamcatcher.* Scholastic, 1992.

Van Allsburg, Chris. *Just a Dream.* Houghton Mifflin, 1990.

Winter, Jeanette. *The Librarian of Basra: A True Story from Iraq.* Harcourt Children's Books, 2005.

Wood, Audrey, and Mark Teague (illustrator). *Sweet Dream Pie.* Scholastic Paperbacks, 2002.

Chapter 4
Tales of Magical Helpers

Stories of enchanted creatures that help people are found all over the world. These include tales of the menehune in Hawaii. Menehune are "little people" living in the woods that do all kinds of nice things when no one's watching. They can be mischievous as well. There are tales of the pookah in Irish folklore who often helps out in the kitchen. The pookah is just one of many Irish magical creatures. Our first story in this chapter is from Sweden and captivates the listeners with the magical feats of ten fairies and the resulting magic in the girl, Inga. This story delights every age group and has everyone looking at their fingers a little bit differently.

Finger Play Warm-Up

Once everyone's hands are in their laps, you may begin the story.

Inga and the Ten Fairy Helpers

Based on a Folktale from Sweden

Once there was a girl named Inga. Inga did not like to work! She was an only child and her parents did everything for her. What did Inga do? **Inga sat, hands in her lap.**

Her mother laced up Inga's shoes while **Inga sat, hands in her lap.** Her father cleared the dinner table while **Inga sat, hands in her lap.**

All the work to be done was done
while **Inga sat, hands in her lap.**

Then, one summer, Inga went to stay with her cousins.
Her cousins did their share of the chores.
But even with their example,
Inga sat, hands in her lap.

But Inga's cousins did not tidy up her room.
Nor did they smooth the spread on her bed.
So Inga's room got very messy.
She didn't like it like that.
But still Inga sat, hands in her lap.

Sitting alone in her messy room, tears filled her eyes and
trickled down her cheeks. Suddenly a strange little man
appeared. He told her that he was her fairy godfather.

"You don't like this messy room, but you don't want to
clean it up, is that right?" he asked.

Inga nodded.

"Well, here are ten little helpers to help you out!"
He snapped his fingers and **ten little fairies appeared.**
They went right to work and, in no time at all, the
room was spotless.

Inga was smiling!

Her fairy godfather said to Inga, **"Take your**
hands out of your lap." She did.
"Now stretch them out," he said. **She did.**

Now he spoke to the helpers,
"Thumb—Hop, Hop!"
And the first helper hopped into Inga's thumb.
"Now you, Old Pointer!"
And the next fairy jumped into her pointer finger.
"Stand tall, Tall One!"
And the third leapt into Inga's middle finger.
"Good Friend, go join her!"
This helper went into her ring finger.
"Little One, have fun, quickly now!"
And the fifth little helper leapt into Inga's little finger.

Her fairy godfather repeated his directions to the other five helpers:
"Thumb—Hop, Hop!"
"Now you, Old Pointer!"
"Stand tall, Tall One!"
"Good Friend, go join her!"
"Little One, have fun, quickly now!"
And they leapt into Inga's other five fingers.

The fairy Godfather added,
"I think that's all you need!"
And he disappeared.

And it was all she needed.
Inga's fingers felt so alive, they couldn't rest in her lap.
She wiggled them around.
They wanted to do something!

So Inga ran downstairs,

set the table,

and straightened the chairs;

cooked the dinner,

and swept the floor;

cleaned the dishes,

and painted the door;

tied her shoes,

and put the tools away.

Then she ran outside with her cousins to play.

And from that day on,

Inga never again sat,

with her hands in her lap.

The End

Storytelling Tips

Younger Children: When Inga discovers the magic in her own hands, instead of the hand-clap rhyme presented in the story, use gestures to show all that Inga does with her hands to help at the table. You can shuffle out plates, scramble the eggs, pour milk while making a gargling sound, and use your hands as bread going in the toaster. Do all the hand moves very quickly—the more animated, the better.

Older Children: For children who play clapping games like "Miss Mary Mack," the closing clap rhythm for Inga's work can be expanded. Unless you're an old hand at this, the children will have more ideas than you could ever invent for great slap–clap routines. Let the students create their own with the words of the story and teach it to you and the others. They can also create their own working slap–clap rhymes for Inga's work.

 LITERACY CONNECTION: Vocabulary. Playing with words and rhythms helps children discover the joy of using words expressively and offers the opportunity to increase their vocabularies.

Any of these approaches describing Inga in action work wonderfully. You should use what is most comfortable for you, because that will be most effective. The process of discovering your own comfort level in telling a story demonstrates the importance of helping children find theirs. With care, this work with stories supports a wide range of learning styles.

In the following tale from West Africa, the magical helpers are children. But they are not children at the beginning of this tale; they are gourds. The theme of the importance of each individual is quite poignant for the older children listeners. The magical help of the little gourds-turned-children will delight the younger girls and boys gathered around you.

The Calabash Children

A Tale from East Africa

There once was a woman who lived by herself in a little house. Her husband had died, and she had no children. She was lonely, but she contented herself working in her garden. She was friendly with her neighbors but had a high fence around her place to keep out animals that might eat the garden. Still she could see the mountain rising up above her fence and she often found herself speaking to the spirit of the mountain, asking for children.

One day she was working in the garden talking as she worked. She always did this. She talked to the vegetables as she worked. In a way, the vegetables were her children. She came to the gourds. 'Well," she said, "You're ready to cut off the vines. I'll let you dry, and you will make wonderful calabash I can sell in the market." She cut a group of gourds off their vines and carried them to her house.

When she got inside, she hung the gourds up to dry on the rafters in the room. "You will make beautiful calabash," she repeated. "There you go, my little ones. You can hang there in my house. Oh, if you were my real children you would swing back and forth, back and forth, filling this room with laughter." The last gourd was just round like a pumpkin. It did not have a neck, so she laid this last gourd by the fire so it could dry out there. "Little one on the ground, if you were my child I would call you Kitete," she said.

The next morning before she left for the market, she looked at the hanging calabash, "Goodbye, my calabash children and my little Kitete on the ground. I will see you when I return from the market." She left the house, went through her gate, latched it, and walked to the village. Well, it seems that the spirit in the mountain had been listening to her because as soon as she left, Kitete, the round calabash on the ground, transformed into a boy who stood up. He then lowered each calabash to the ground. When they touched the ground, they became girls and boys. They ran outside to play. Kitete moved a little slower. He watched his sisters and brothers playing. He smiled.

The calabash children played and laughed and danced around. After a while they went to work. They cleaned the little house; they worked in the garden; and they gathered wood. Just before the old woman returned, they ran inside where Kitete, the quiet boy had gone back to sit by the fire. He lifted them up to the rafters. As soon as they grabbed the rafters, the children turned back into calabash. The woman returned. When she opened the gate, she wondered where the stacked wood had come from. She gazed at the weeded garden, and when she stepped inside, she was amazed at how beautiful her house looked.

She went back outside and over to one of the neighbor's houses. The neighbor smiled and told her that he had not done any work there, but had heard children laughing and playing on the other side of the fence. The woman looked at her neighbor in amazement. "Children?" she asked. "I have no children!" She went back home and fixed her supper. As she lay down in her bed, she called out, "Goodnight my calabash children."

The next day, the woman had to go to a neighboring village, and so she bid her calabash children a good day, went through the gate, and was on her way. Once again Kitete lowered his sisters and brothers to the ground. Once again they worked and played, and he sat by the fire until it was time to return to the rafters. Once again the woman was puzzled and asked her neighbors, who again said that they heard children working and playing.

The next day, she announced to the calabash children that she was going to the village, but she didn't. She closed the gate like always. She walked down the road for a few minutes and then turned back around. She walked to a spot next to her fence where she could peer through. She saw her calabash children playing in the yard. Their clothes were the color of the gourds they had been. She opened the gate and ran in. The children scurried into the house where Kitete stood and began to lift one of his sisters to the rafter. "Stop!" cried the woman, "Please stay. Be my children! Don't turn back. You *are* my calabash children. You have always been." And so the calabash children stayed as children and the woman was happy.

Time went by and the calabash children played and worked and the woman had more time to enjoy her life. But Kitete never left the fire. Now that he no longer had the job of lifting his sisters and brothers up and down from the rafters, he did nothing at all. He just sat by the fire and ate quietly with the rest of the family. Every day, the woman watched her other children working and playing and Kitete doing nothing at all. It began to irritate her that Kitete did nothing but sit by the fire and eat meals. One day she tripped over him and fell to the ground. She looked and Kitete and yelled, "You do nothing. You are worthless! Why did you even become a person in the first place?" Then she stopped. "Oh no!" she cried out as she watched Kitete turn back into a calabash lying next to the fire. The woman stood up. She listened. There was no laughter coming from outside the house. She ran out. Here and there, scattered across the yard were the calabash children, calabash once again.

The woman sadly picked up the calabash and carried them inside. She hung them up on the rafters. She cried, but it did no good. They would not be children again. She looked at the round one on the ground, the one who had made it all possible. She picked up that calabash, Kitete, and held it on her lap in front of the fire. She stared into the fire filled with sorrow.

The End

Activity: Acting out Part of the Story (Pre-K–Grade 1)

Instead of acting out the entire tale, you may want to use this story as a cleanup activity. Invite the boys and girls to join you for a story before they have put away things from another project. Then when you reach the part of the story where the gourds have once again changed into children and the old woman is about to leave the house you can say, "Would you like to be the kids cleaning up while I go away?" Generally this idea will excite your young listeners. (If their teacher is present, you can have her leave for the cleanup. Let her know when to return and tell her the lines to say.) Then come back saying, "I wonder what that noise is coming over my fence!" All the children will run back to their listening positions. They can repeat the acting out of the playing and working in the next section of the story as well. In this activity, no one plays Kitete; everyone is one of the working children. They will continue to come back from their play and cleaning up to hear the next part of the tale. When the old woman gets mad and yells at Kitete, all the children listeners will be seated and will experience that terrible moment. They generally become very quiet.

Afterward you can talk about the ending and how it made them feel. They will have many suggestions for different endings to this story.

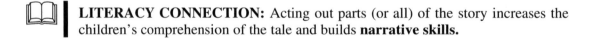 **LITERACY CONNECTION:** Acting out parts (or all) of the story increases the children's comprehension of the tale and builds **narrative skills.**

The Skeleton for "The Calabash Children"

1. An old woman lives alone, wishing she had children.

2. She cuts some gourds and hangs them from her rafters.

3. One gourd does not have a neck, so it lies on the floor.

4. When the woman goes to the village, Kitete, the gourd/calabash on the floor, becomes a boy.

5. He lowers the other calabash. They become children.

6. They play and do work in the garden and clean her house.

7. She comes home.

8. They become gourds again.

9. This repeats.

10. She acts like she is leaving and sees them through fence.

11. She begs them to stay as children. They do.

12. Time goes by.

13. Kitete always sits by fire; he never plays or works.

14. The woman trips over Kitete and angrily berates him.

15. Kitete becomes a gourd again.

16. The other children become gourds again.

17. The woman is alone.

The End

From *Stories in Action: Interactive Tales and Learning Activities to Promote Early Literacy*
by Bill Gordh. Westport, CT: Libraries Unlimited. Copyright © 2006.

Activity: Creating a Magical Helper (All Ages)

Ask each student to imagine a magical helper to do a particular chore. They should think of a name for it, what it looks like, what it can do, and how it accomplishes its task. When they have their ideas worked out, each should make a "thumbs-up" signal to show he or she is ready. Then have the children take turns talking about their magical helper. Second, third, and fourth graders can also draw the helper. Discuss which helpers might team up. As a group, create a story of the magical helpers working with a boy and girl to accomplish some difficult task. Depending on the size of the group, you might divide the group into smaller groups and then each smaller group can share the story they create. Some models for this kind of story include the folktale "The 5 Chinese Brothers" and the Grimm Brothers' story "The Six Servants."

Thematic Picture Book Suggestions

 LITERACY CONNECTION: Print motivation: After exploring the stories and activities about magical helpers in this chapter, the children will be intrigued by books that further the exploration.

dePaola, Tomie. *Jamie O'Rourke and the Pooka*. Puffin Books, Reprint, 2002.

Grimm, Jacob, and Jim (illustrator). *The Elves and the Shoemaker*. Chronicle Books, 2003.

Van Allsburg, Chris. *The Widow's Broom*. Houghton Mifflin, 1992.

Chapter 5
Tales of Sharing

Deciding to share or trying not to has been a theme in folktales all over the world. Most humans have a difficulty with sharing, and it is a major issue throughout childhood and into adulthood too (if we'd admit it). Hearing stories about the difficulty of sharing makes children aware that they are not alone in these mixed feelings of knowing what they should do and feeling what they want to do. The stories provide a great springboard for discussion. The finger play that follows also points out how each person's actions in a group can make a big difference.

Finger Play Warm-Up

When the story describes Noora taking the cup and pot of honey out of the cupboard, invite the children to join you and take out their cups and honey as well. It is likely that they will be doing the finger play anyway, but sometimes they get so involved listening to the story that they stop using their hands.

The Honey Pot

A Folktale from the Middle East

A long time ago, there lived a king in a small village. His birthday was coming soon and everyone in the village was talking about it.

But what should they give their King?
A man suggested, "How about a horse?"

They all shook their heads.
No, the King had the most beautiful horses in the land.

A woman called out, "How about a goat?
It will bring the King's family milk and cheese."
They all shook their heads.
The king had hundreds of goats already.

"How about honey?"
asked a girl named Noora.

"Honey?!" said everyone. "Why honey?"

"Well," replied Noora, "The King loves honey, and
if each of us gave a cup, we could fill a huge pot, and
it would last him for years and years."

The rest of the townspeople looked at one another
and started smiling and nodding. They liked this idea!

The people dragged a huge pot to the center of the
village. Then everyone went home to get their cups
of honey.

When Noora got home, **she opened her cupboard
and got out her cup. Then she took out her little
pot of honey.** Oh, how Noora loved honey! In fact she
loved honey so much she did not want to give any of it
away. She thought about it.

There were many people in her village. Each
person would pour a cup of honey into the
big pot.

Noora got an idea. If she put water in her cup
instead of honey, no one would ever know.
The King certainly wouldn't notice a little water
in all of that honey!

**Noora quickly put her little honey pot back on
the shelf** and **filled her cup with water.**

Then she went with her cup and stood in line
with everyone else. Noora watched as one by one,
the villagers emptied their cups into the great big pot.
Now it was Noora's turn. **She emptied her cup
into the pot, too.**

Then the villagers invited the King to come and
see his birthday present.

The King arrived. He looked at the full pot in
front of him. He looked out across the crowd.
They all shouted, "It's honey!" He smiled, **dipped
his finger into the pot** and **took a taste.**

He looked up with a strange expression on his face.
"Is this a joke?" he asked.
The people shook their heads. The King cried,
"This pot is full of water!"

All the villagers stared at their King.

What could have happened? Can you guess?
Well, if you guessed that all the villagers had the
same idea as the young girl Noora, you would be
right. Everyone in the village had filled their cups
with water, too!

The End

Storytelling Tips (All Ages)

When you ask, "What could have happened?" take time to listen to a number of suggestions. Knowing that everyone put water in the pot makes it seem like that's the only possibility, but often children come up with a variety of possible reasons. If they joined you in the finger play when Noora put water in her cup, they have already enacted what all the villagers did! A discussion can follow about sharing and the importance of everyone doing their part in a group.

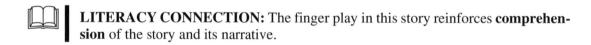

LITERACY CONNECTION: The finger play in this story reinforces **comprehension** of the story and its narrative.

This little story from Greece uses a familiar structure of three siblings setting out on a mission. The third (and youngest in this case) accomplishing what the other two cannot is part of the same structure (consider "The Three Little Pigs" and "The Three Billy Goat's Gruff") . In this story, however, the interesting twist on the regular "threes" story is that listeners do not realize the failure of the first two until the end of the story. The theme of the importance of sharing with those less fortunate is always worth a visit.

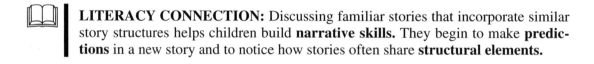

LITERACY CONNECTION: Discussing familiar stories that incorporate similar story structures helps children build **narrative skills.** They begin to make **predictions** in a new story and to notice how stories often share **structural elements.**

The Three Brothers

A Tale from Greece

There were not many paying jobs near their home, so three brothers set out together to find work. They carried one loaf of bread with them to share if they got hungry, and they began walking. They walked all morning, and at noon they found a nice shady tree along the road. They sat down on the grass under the tree to break their bread and drink some water. An old man came hobbling down the road and stopped when he saw the three brothers.

The old man smiled at the three brothers and asked if he could sit with them. They said, "Sure. Sit down." After the old man sat down, they passed their loaf of bread to him. He looked at the three brothers, "Isn't this all the bread you have?"

"Yes," they replied, "But you look hungry and you should break off as much as you need."

The old man smiled again. "Thank you," he said and broke off a piece of bread. "You are very generous to share your bread with a stranger," he added. As the old man and the brothers ate their bread and sipped their water, they talked. When they were finished, the old man asked if he could walk with them.

Together they walked down the road, the three brothers and the old man. They stopped again when the old man got tired. The old man asked the oldest brother, "If you could have a wish right now, what would it be?" The brother looked around as he thought. He saw beautiful hills spotted with bushes. The bushes made him think of sheep. The oldest brother replied, "My wish would be that all the bushes on this hillside would become sheep and they would be my sheep, and these would be my fields. I would become a shepherd."

The old man nodded and then asked, "And would you share with those who were not so lucky as you?"

"Of course!" replied the oldest brother. The old man snapped his fingers three times—SNAP, SNAP, SNAP—and the bushes turned into sheep. "There you go," said the old man.

The oldest brother thanked the old man and ran up the hillside to gather and count his sheep. The two other brothers and the old man continued down the road. After a while, the old man asked the second brother, "If you could have any wish at all, what would it be?"

The second brother thought about it and as he thought, he gazed at the hillside. "If I had a wish, I would wish that this hillside was covered with olive trees and the olive orchard would be mine to gather and sell olives and make olive oil."

"And if your wish came true," continued the old man, "would you share with those who were poor and not so lucky as you?"

"Of course!" answered the second brother. "Very well," said the old man and he snapped his fingers three times—SNAP, SNAP, SNAP—and the hillside was covered with olive trees.

The second brother smiled and exclaimed, "Oh, thank you!" to the old man as he ran up the hill to look over his new orchard full of ripe green olives.

The youngest brother and the old man continued walking. After a while they stopped again and this time the old man asked the youngest, "What wish would you make?"

The youngest brother looked around and noticed a beautiful spring bubbling with fresh water just off the road. "Well," he replied, "I would wish that the spring there flowed with honey. Then I would set up a little honey shop right here along the road."

"And if your wish came true," asked the old man, "would you share with those who were poor and not so lucky as you?"

"Of course," replied the youngest brother, "I would always share with others." The old man smiled and snapped his fingers three times—SNAP, SNAP, SNAP—and the spring flowed with honey.

Time passed.

One day the youngest brother was standing in front of his honey shop when an old man came up and asked, "Will you give a taste of honey to a poor old man?"

The brother smiled at the old man and said, "Of course! Sit on the bench here and rest. I'll be right back." The brother went into his shop and came back with some honey for the old man, and it was spread on a nice roll.

"Oh thank you!" said the old man. The brother watched the old man eating the bread and honey and remembered. He was the same old man who had snapped his fingers those many years before. The old man nodded, "Yes, it's me all right, and I'm glad to see you doing so well. How are your brothers?"

The youngest brother shook his head, "I'm not sure. I have been so busy here I have not seen them for a long time. I would imagine they are doing fine after your generosity!"

The old man looked at the young man and said, "Let's take a walk and see for ourselves."

"OK!" said the brother and they walked down the road where they had walked together those years before. They came to the hills where his brother's olive orchard had sprouted but the hills were covered with brambles. The youngest brother shook his head. "What happened to the olives?" he wondered.

They walked on. They came to the pastures where the sheep had appeared, but there were no sheep, only bushes. The youngest brother shook his head. "What happened to the sheep?" he wondered. No olives! No sheep. What happened? Then he had an idea, "I bet they didn't share."

He turned to ask the old man if he was right, but the old man had disappeared.

The End

Story Activity: Children Making Wishes (All Ages)

After "sharing" this story, revisit the structure of the tale. Ask how the brothers came to their wish ideas. Someone will point out that each of the three brothers looked around him for inspiration. Have each child take a look out the window and think of a wish based on something she or he sees. Pretend the whole group is traveling with the old man and each in turn can offer his or her wish. You have just provided a model for finding story ideas.

 LITERACY CONNECTION: The discussion and experience of using surroundings as a springboard for story creations will have an ongoing positive effect in building **narrative skills.**

The Skeleton for "The Three Brothers"

1. Three Brothers set off to find work.

2. They stop for lunch on side of road.

3. An old man asks to join them. They say he may.

4. The three brothers and old man walk together.

5. The old man asks oldest brother what he would wish for.

6. The brother says that he wishes the field were full of sheep, his sheep.

7. The old man asks if the brother would share with the needy. Yes.

8. The wish comes true.

9. Two brothers and the old man walk on.

10. Same question to second brother.

11. Second brother wishes the hillsides were covered with olive bushes—his.

12. The old man asks if he would share. Yes.

13. The wish comes true.

14. The youngest brother and the old man walk.

15. The old man asks the youngest brother what he wishes for.

16. The youngest brother says he wishes the spring would flow with honey and he could sell it.

17. The old man asks about sharing with the needy. Yes, replies the brother.

18. The spring flows with honey.

19. The years go by.

20. The old man comes by the honey stand.

21. The young man and old man walk to see how the brothers are doing.

22. There are no olives. No sheep.

23. The other two brothers did not share.

The End

From *Stories in Action: Interactive Tales and Learning Activities to Promote Early Literacy* by Bill Gordh. Westport, CT: Libraries Unlimited. Copyright © 2006.

Storytellers often use the term "sharing" for what they do when they tell stories. The idea of "sharing a story" suggests that instead of the teller and listeners being on two ends of the telling of a tale, that there is a dialogue (mostly silent) between teller and listener. A tale often changes during the telling according to the way the listeners are responding. This is one of the reasons for the story skeletons in this book—they allow tellers to be flexible as the story progresses.

The following story from Korea describes the dangers of not sharing stories that you have heard and loved. I often use it at the close of a residency to encourage the children to share the stories they have heard.

The Story Bag

A Tale from Korea

Once there was a boy who loved stories. Everyone he met he asked to tell him a story. He loved stories so much, he kept a bag tied to his belt where he saved his stories and at night before bed, he'd open his story bag and listen to one of his favorites again. He lived in a big house, and one of the servants who worked for his family always had a tale for the story-hungry boy.

This boy who loved stories grew up, and at the time of the telling of this tale, he is preparing for his wedding. Soon he will mount his horse and ride to the house of his bride-to-be, and they will be married. His own house is filled with people helping prepare for the big day. The servant who had always told stories to the boy is now an old man but still helping whenever he can. He was in the kitchen when he heard a strange sound coming from the little hall near the kitchen door. It sounded like tiny voices muttering!

The old servant walked back into the hall and hanging from one of the coat hooks he saw a little bag—the story bag! It must have been hanging there for years! There was noise coming from the bag, and when the old servant leaned over with his ear close, he could hear the stories talking. They were angry! They were mad that the boy had forgotten them. Now he was getting married and they would never be heard again! The old servant listened more closely. What he heard next really made him nervous. One story said, "I know what I'll do. I'll turn into a bush with poison red berries and plant myself near the road he will travel on. When he sees me, he will become so hungry, he will climb off his horse and eat my berries. Then he will die!"

Another story piped up, "Good. If that doesn't work, I will be a poison spring along the way. When he sees me, he will become so thirsty, he will climb off his horse and take a drink. Then he will die!" "Excellent!" cheered another story, "And if that doesn't work, I'll be a sharp piece of glass hidden in the straw. When he climbs off his horse, he will step on me and I will go through his foot! Blood will cover the ground." Another story had an idea and spoke, "And if he makes it to the bridal chamber, I will be a ball of poisonous snakes hidden under the bed covers. When he climbs into bed, he will die!"

The old servant could not believe it! He looked out the window. The young man was just climbing on his horse! The old man thought fast. He hurried outside, "Master, master, let me lead your horse to your bride's home."

The young man smiled, but shook his head, "Oh that's all right. I think I'm old enough to ride a horse by myself."

The old man insisted, "Oh please, one last time. Just like when you were a little boy." "All right," said the young man, "One last time."

So the old servant led the horse down the road. They traveled up over a hill and down the other side. There on the side of the road was a bush laden with ripe red berries. The young man saw the berries. He was hungry.

He called to the old man, "Old man, whoa!" The old man pretended he did not understand and said, "Whoa? No, don't worry. I did not slow down. I won't whoa!" and kept walking.

"No!" cried the young man, "No, whoa!"

"No whoa?" responded the old man, "All right, no whoa, I will not stop. I know you are in a hurry." The young man just shook his head as they left the berry bush behind.

Soon they were passing the little spring of cool water. It made the young man thirsty and once again he tried to get the old man to stop. Once again, the old man pretended not to understand and kept going. When they arrived at his bride's house, the bride and her family were waiting standing at the top of a few stone steps. The young man stopped his horse just before the steps and began to climb off. The glass was waiting beneath the straw, but the old man elbowed the horse so that it bucked and threw the young man onto the ground behind the horse. The young man jumped up dusting himself off and gave the old servant a furious look, but his bride was waiting, so he went to join her.

The wedding took place and the groom and his new bride were finally alone in the bridal chamber. Well, they thought they were alone, but as soon as they had closed the door, the old servant stepped out from behind a curtain. Before the astonished groom could utter a word, the old servant took his large sword and chopped the bed in half! There on the bed was a ball of poisonous snakes cut in half!

The young man was shaking his head. He asked the servant what was going on. The old servant told him all about the stories and their plans.

"Oh," said the young man, "my stories, my wonderful stories. How could I have ever forgotten about them? I will make them happy again and before too long share those stories with my own children!"

The End

Activity: Creating a Story Bag (All Ages)

Have the children think about having story bags of their own. With the younger children, go around the circle asking the children to name one story that is in their bag. Make the rounds a few times. Real Story Bags can be made and objects or pictures of objects that remind prereaders of stories can be dropped in. For example, one of the color counting bears could be put in a bag for "The Three Bears," or a picture of a jar of honey could be the reminder for "The Honey Pot." For early readers the titles of the stories (or story objects or pictures if they prefer) can be put in the bag. Story objects can still be fun for third or fourth graders. You can also generate a list of stories from the whole group. Each child should then pick one story out of the Story Bag and tell it at home that night. After a few times, they might take the Story Bags home and let one of their parents pick an object out of the bag, then the child tells the story. If you decide to do this, a letter explaining the activity should accompany the child.

 LITERACY CONNECTION: Providing a concrete inspiration (like a Story Bag with objects) for telling stories often gives children the extra "something" they need to discover the joys of telling a tale and builds **narrative skills.**

The Skeleton for "The Story Bag"

1. A boy loves stories and collects them in a story bag.

2. The boy grows up and forgets about bag and stories.

3. He is getting married and traveling to his bride's house for wedding.

4. An old servant hears stories in bag plotting to kill the young man.

5. One story will become poison berries.

6. One story will become a poisonous spring.

7. One story will become sharp glass on the ground.

8. One story will become a ball of poison snakes and hide in the bridal chamber bed.

9. The old man leads the young man on his horse to bride's.

10. The young man wants to stop, but the old man keeps going past dangers.

11. The old man makes the horse buck to avoid glass.

12. The old man chops snakes in half in the bridal bed.

13. The servant explains to the young man that the stories were angry.

14. The young man plans to start sharing stories again.

The End

From *Stories in Action: Interactive Tales and Learning Activities to Promote Early Literacy*
by Bill Gordh. Westport, CT: Libraries Unlimited. Copyright © 2006.

Other stories in this book about sharing include "Coyote and the Meat" (Chapter 3) and "Spider at Hawk's Feast" (Chapter 7). Following are some picture books that will also further an exploration of this theme.

Thematic Picture Book Suggestions

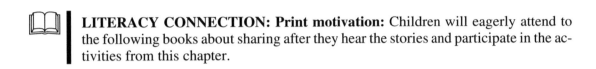 **LITERACY CONNECTION: Print motivation:** Children will eagerly attend to the following books about sharing after they hear the stories and participate in the activities from this chapter.

Cooney, Barbara. *Miss Rumphius.* Puffin Books (reprint ed.), 1985.

dePaola, Tomie. *The Legend of the Bluebonnet: An Old Tale of Texas.* Putnam Publishing Group (re-issue ed.), 1992.

Faulkner, William J., and Roberta Wilson (illustrator). *Brer Tiger and the Big Wind.* HarperCollins, 1995.

Wood, Audrey, and Don Wood (illustrator). *The Little Mouse, The Red Ripe Strawberry and the Hungry Bear.* Child's Play International, 1984.

Chapter 6
Tales of Inanimate Objects Animating

This is an unusual chapter theme but one that will spark the imaginations of all who hear the stories. They are fun to hear and to act out; they provide another direction to explore when creating original stories. The finger play that begins this chapter is a story from China.

Finger Play Warm-Up

 With younger children, you can follow the warm-up by enacting and singing the old nursery rhyme, "I'm a Little Teapot."

I'm a Little Teapot

I'm a little teapot

Short and stout

Here is my handle

Here is my spout

When I get all steamed up

Hear me shout

"Tip me over

And pour me out!"

Then you can begin the story.
Have older listeners make the teapot when you do.

The Clay Teapot Takes Charge

A Folktale from China

This story has no people.
But this story has a house.
And one day in this house, **the clay teapot took charge.**

Standing on the shelf, she called in her helpers:
Needle, Onion, Fly, Mudpie, and Rice Flour.
Then she gave out the orders:

"Needle, sweep the floor!

Onion, bring the cow home!

Fly, herd in the ox!

Mudpie, fetch the water!

Rice Flour, check the weather!"

Then Clay Teapot sat up on the shelf waiting
for the work to be done.

Well, her friends tried; but this is what happened.

When Needle went to sweep the floor,
What happened?
It slipped and fell into a crack.

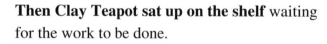

When Onion tried to lead the cow home,
What happened?
The cow was hungry and gobbled it up.

When Fly started to drive in the ox,
What happened?
With a swing of its tail, the ox sent the fly
high into the clouds.

When Mudpie carried the bucket,
What happened?
Some of the water sloshed out and turned Mudpie into just
plain old mud.

And when Rice Flour climbed onto the roof
to check the weather,
What happened?
The wind blew it in a hundred different directions.

Now all this time the clay teapot was waiting
patiently, but after waiting and waiting and waiting,
she decided to see what was going on.
So Clay Teapot jumped off the shelf to the ground.
What happened?
She had forgotten she was made of clay, and
she shattered into thousands of little pieces.

It was a bad-luck day for that household!

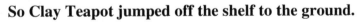

The End

Storytelling Tips (All Ages)

You can enlist the children to shout out "What happened?" to help you tell the story. This energizes the experience and makes them excited about hearing what happens to each of these unfortunate characters.

Activity: Acting out the Story (Pre-K–Grade 1)

This is a good story for this activity because the children love to play these inanimate objects as they come to life. It can be quite hilarious. Guide the activity as you have for the other stories. Then ask the children to remind you of the rules:

1. Listen to the storyteller.

2. Be safe.

3. Have fun!

Then retell the tale as the children act it out.

You may find that some children don't want to have something bad happen to their characters. You can generally keep everyone happy by making the story even more comical with your tone of voice and speed of delivery. You can challenge and applaud each of the characters for making a funny fall. (This same technique works for characters dying in stories. There are not any dying characters in this book, but you may run into the situation when children act out other stories.)

Activity: Children Presenting the Tale as a Group (Grades 2–4)

This is a fun story for the children to tell. One (or more) person can be the narrator, another the teapot. (Another option is for you to be the narrator.) When Teapot calls in the helpers, each of the characters echoes her call, for example, Teapot says, "Needle!" Then the child playing Needle stands at attention and says, "Needle!" The noncharacter performers call out "What happened?" Then the character tells what happens or acts it out (or both). You can try this in a number of ways, and the boys and girls can discuss and choose the best way for them to present the story to other groups.

 LITERACY CONNECTION: The active participation of the children in the discussion of how to present a tale makes them more aware of how the story works and also builds their **narrative skills.** The retelling strategies they develop here can be used often and refined as they work with more stories.

This hilarious tale from Africa presents a lot of unusual characters that talk! It is a cumulative tale that you can visit again when you are exploring that structure in Chapter 13.

The Talking Yam

A Tale from West Africa

Dig, dig, dig

Digging with the Digging stick

Dig, dig, dig

Digging with the Digging stick

Ashante [pronunciation: Ah–SHAN–tay) was working in his garden.

Dig, dig, dig

Digging with the Digging stick

Dig, dig, dig—

Ashante stopped! He heard a voice. It was a yam talking! A talking yam!

It said, "Yaah! Don't dig, dig, dig me with that digging stick!"

"Ahh!" screamed the farmer, "Did you hear that?" he asked of no one in particular.

"Of course! Er-ruff!" answered his dog, "The yam wants you to leave it alone. So stop digging!"

"A talking dog now!" howled the farmer. "I'll teach you to be more polite." Ashante broke a branch off the tree.

The tree spoke, "Don't use my branch to hit your dog!"

"Ahh!" screeched Ashante and dropped the branch. Ashante went running.

He ran 'til he came to his friend, Amadou (Ah-MAH-doo), the fisherman. Amadou was repairing his fish trap. He looked up and asked, "What's wrong Ashante?"

"What's wrong? I was hoeing my field when a yam called out, 'Stop digging' and then my dog spoke and said, 'Stop digging' and a tree said, 'Don't hit your dog with my branch!' so I started running.

"That can't be true," said Amadou.

His fish trap spoke, "Sure it's true. The yam doesn't want to be hurt." Amadou dropped his talking fish trap, jumped up, and the two friends started running.

They ran 'til they came to their friend Abene (Ah-BEN-ay). They stopped when they saw her. They were panting. "What's wrong?" asked Abene.

"What's wrong?!" exclaimed Ashante, "I was hoeing my field when a yam called out, 'Stop digging' and then my dog spoke and said, 'Stop digging' and a tree said, 'Don't hit your dog with my branch!' so I started running."

"And then," added Amadou, "when Ashante told me his story, my fish trap said, 'The yam doesn't want to be hurt.' "

Abene smiled and shook her head, "I think the heat has gotten to both of you."

Abene's head cloth spoke up, "They're not making it up. The yam just wants to grow in peace."

Abene pulled the head wrap off her head and threw it to the ground. Now all three friends were running. They ran 'til they came to the river. There they saw their friend Enenge (Eh-NEN-gay) bathing in the river, "What's wrong? Why are you running?"

"What's wrong?!" exclaimed Ashante, "I was hoeing my field when a yam called out, 'Stop digging' and then my dog spoke and said, 'Stop digging' and a tree said, "Don't hit your dog with my branch!' so I started running."

"And then," added Amadou, "when Ashante told me his story, my fish trap said, 'The yam doesn't want to be hurt.' "

"And then," added Abene, "My head cloth said, 'The yam just wants to grow in peace.' "

Enenge looked at his friends, "Come in the river. You need to relax." The river spoke, "I'm not surprised that they're excited."

The three friends did not enter the river. Enenge jumped out and all four friends ran until they came to the village and did not stop until they found the chief. The chief was sitting on his stool. He looked up. "What's wrong?" asked the chief.

"What's wrong?!" exclaimed Ashante, "I was hoeing my field when a yam called out, 'Stop digging' and then my dog spoke and said, 'Stop digging' and a tree said, 'Don't hit your dog with my branch!' so I started running."

"And then," added Amadou, "when Ashante told me his story, my fish trap said, 'The yam doesn't want to be hurt.' "

"And then," added Abene, "My head cloth said, 'The yam just wants to grow in peace.' "

And Enenge spoke up, "And I was in the river and the river said, 'I'm not surprised that they're excited.' "

The chief looked at the four friends and spoke, "That is enough! You're going to upset everyone with your nonsense. Now leave and go back to your work."

The chief watched as the four friends slowly walked back through the village. The chief's stool spoke up, "Isn't that something—a talking yam?"

The End

 LITERACY CONNECTION: The West African names in this story may be unfamiliar to some of the children. Telling the story provides the opportunity to begin building **phonological awareness** and cultural **vocabularies.**

Activity: Acting out the Story (All Ages)

This activity is generally aimed at younger children, but the story is such a hoot that any of your children will have fun acting it out. It is such a wild idea that some boys and girls who might not usually participate will join in. In addition to the children choosing their parts and finding places around the "Acting-out space" you may want to map out the enactment together. Discuss where each of the characters will be and how the people will move from one to the next. Who will be the river? How will you show "river-ness"? Will someone play the stool of the chief? This is a great story to use as a problem-solving task. For this story, the whole group might create a story skeleton or you may want to use the one presented here and add some details to it.

 LITERACY CONNECTION: To figure out how to enact a story, the children must examine it carefully. This makes them aware of how the **story is structured** and builds **narrative skills.**

The Skeleton for "The Talking Yam"

1. Ashante in his garden digging up yams.

2. Yam says not to dig him up.

3. Ashante can't believe it.

4. Dog tells him to leave the yam alone.

5. Ashante can't believe his dog is talking.

6. Ashante goes for a branch to hit his dog.

7. Tree says not to use its branch to hit the dog.

8. Ashante runs away, running until he comes to the fisherman Amadou.

9. Amadou asks what's wrong. Ashante tells him what happened.

10. Amadou doesn't believe it. Fish trap says it's true.

11. Ashante and Amadou run until they come to Abene.

12. They tell her what happened. She doesn't believe.

13. Her head wrap speaks and says it believes.

14. The three friends go running until they meet Enenge bathing in the river.

15. They tell him. Enenge tells them to calm down.

16. The river speaks.

17. The four friends run until they come to the chief.

18. They tell the chief their story.

19. He dismisses the whole story and tells them to leave.

20. The chief's stool says it's surprising that the yam talked.

The End

From *Stories in Action: Interactive Tales and Learning Activities to Promote Early Literacy*
by Bill Gordh. Westport, CT: Libraries Unlimited. Copyright © 2006.

It seems only fitting that such an adventurous chapter should close with another animated clay pot story. The pot in this tale, however, is not a teapot, just a cooking pot and the ending is joyful. There are many versions of this ancient tale from South America, many of which have the household objects animating during an eclipse and reeking havoc. In this version, they just have fun.

The Clay Pot's Party
A Tale from Bolivia

Long ago, the people did not know it, but all the pots and other household items could move around. Not only could they move around, they could sing and dance. One day when the man who lived in the house was away, the pots decided to have a party. They told everyone else—that is, all the other things in the house—and they went down to the river to get some water. Then they went into the field and got some maize—corn.

They brought the maize back and brewed up a little *chicha,* a delicious corn drink that has been made for hundreds of years. Now it was their turn. Once the *chicha* was ready, they were ready—to have their party! They danced and sang and danced all day until all the *chicha* was gone and they were tired. Then they cleaned themselves up and returned to their places.

Just about then, the door opened and the man came in. He did not notice a thing, for to him everything looked just as it did when he left. But the pots were smiling!

The End

Activity: Acting out the Story (Pre-K–Grade 1)

This is a great companion piece to the opening story of this chapter. The children enjoy playing their characters having a party.

Activity: Playing a Game Based on the Story (Pre-K–Grade 1)

Following the acting-out activity, you can turn part of the tale into a story game. In the game, you become the owner of the house. Then you leave and everyone starts to party. You pretend that you forgot something and have to return. The characters quickly return to their household positions. Whomever you see still moving joins you as the house owner. Rather than kicking the child out of the game, as in Musical Chairs, this allows everyone to play for the whole game. Keep playing until everyone is the owner. A variation to use for the very youngest is to let everyone stay as objects and they just enjoy playing the animated objects and freezing.

The Skeleton for "The Clay Pot's Party"

1. A man leaves his house.

2. The pots and other household objects decide to have a party.

3. They go to the river for water.

4. They go to the field for maize.

5. They make a drink—*chicha*.

6. They have a dancing party.

7. They finish their party, clean up, and return to their spots.

8. The man comes home.

9. Everything seems the same.

10. The pots are smiling.

The End

Activity: Creating Stories with Inanimate Objects Animating (Grades 2–4)

After sharing the two household items stories with the group, create a story together using the inanimate object animating.

- One student suggests a household object.

- The next tells how it animates and what it does.

- The next offers another object to join the story.

- The next tells what these two do, and so on.

 LITERACY CONNECTION: Building the **narrative powers** of the whole group as a group supports each of the individuals. The "leaders" offer models for the children who are more unsure, strengthening both ends of the confidence spectrum.

In Chapter 8, you'll find another story, "The Wild Cherry Tree," in which a tomato, an onion, and a chili pepper get into the action.

Thematic Picture Book Suggestions

 LITERACY CONNECTION: Print motivation. The tales and activities in this chapter about inanimate objects animating get the boys and girls excited about finding stories in books that explore some of the same ideas.

Aylesworth, Jim, and Wendy Anderson Halperin (illustrator). *Full Belly Bowl.* Atheneum, 1999.

Hodges, Margaret, Lafcadio Hearn, and Aki Sogabe (illustrator). *The Boy Who Drew Cats.* Holiday House, 2002.

Partridge, Elizabeth, and Aki Sogabe (illustrator). *Kogi's Mysterious Journey.* Dutton, 2003.

Ransome, Arthur, and Uri Shulevitz (illustrator). *The Fool of the World and the Flying Ship: A Russian Tale.* Farrar, Straus & Giroux, 1987.

Sans Souci, Robert D., and Jerry Pinkney (illustrator). *The Talking Eggs.* Dial, 1989.

Part Two

Exploring Character through Stories

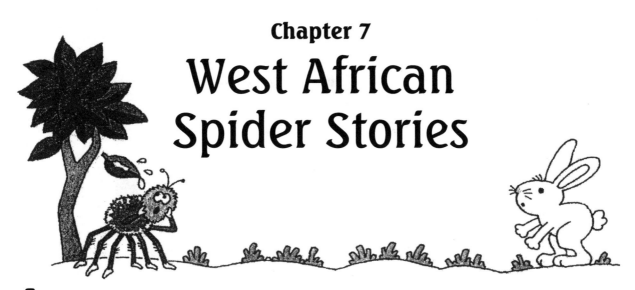

Chapter 7
West African Spider Stories

Anancy (or Anansi) the Spider crawls through many of the best-loved African folktales. The humor in the stories and the delight the spider takes in his tricks delights listeners as well. The fact that the trickster often winds up getting tricked gives the children something to think about. As is the way with all good stories told well, the children become totally involved and learn from the engagement. The first story in this chapter is one the children will learn and want to retell many times. It can also be used as part of the "Why" story exploration in Chapter 12.

Finger Play Warm-Up

Before starting the story, make a crooked-legged spider with your hand and run it around in the air in front of you. Invite the children to make their own spiders. Then tell them that in this story, Spider has long straight legs and to make their spider with long straight legs. Then you can begin. When you introduce the rabbit, they will know they can join in on the rabbit finger play as well.

> **LITERACY CONNECTION:** Using hand gestures that the children can join in on helps them internalize the **structure** of the story and build **narrative skills.**

Why Spider Has Crooked Legs

A Folktale from Liberia

A long time ago, **Spider had long, straight legs and ran about** with his body high off the ground.

Spider did not like to work. When a drought came and there was not much food, Spider didn't even bother leaving his house.

Now **Rabbit** was not this way at all. She was a hard worker. **Every day she went out looking for food for her family.**

One day, Rabbit was hopping along when she smelled a wonderful smell coming over a wall. **She hopped up onto the wall** and **down to the ground on the other side.** There she saw a big tree with **huge petals.** The petals were filled with steaming stew. Ooooh! Did it smell good!

Rabbit sang gently to the tree, "Oh beautiful, wonderful, sweet-smelling tree, would you, could you, would you please **drop one little petal** down to me—just enough for my family?"

As soon as the song was complete, **a petal full of stew came floating gently down, down, down to the ground,** right in front of Rabbit's feet.

Rabbit thanked the tree, **took a little taste** and **hurried home** to her family to share the delicious stew.

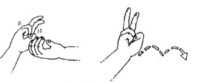

After that, every day **Rabbit went back, hopped up onto the wall and over it**. Then she sang, "Oh beautiful, wonderful, sweet-smelling tree, would you, could you, would you please **drop one little petal** down to me—just enough for my family?"

And as soon as the song was complete, **a petal full of stew came floating down, down, down to the ground,** right in front of Rabbit's feet. Rabbit's family had plenty to eat.

Now one day, **Rabbit ran right into Spider on her way home.** Spider asked, "Where did you get that steaming stew?"

Rabbit said, "Follow me!"

Spider followed Rabbit. **Rabbit hopped up onto the wall and over it.**
Spider jumped up onto the wall and down to the ground next to Rabbit.
Spider listened as Rabbit sang, "Oh beautiful, wonderful, sweet-smelling tree, would you, could you, would you please **drop one little petal** down to me—just enough for my family?"

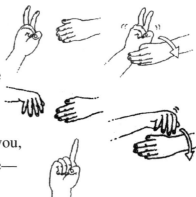

A little petal full of steaming stew floated gently **down, down, down to Rabbit's feet.** Rabbit thanked the tree. Now it was Spider's turn.

Spider did not feel like singing a sweet song and he was very hungry and wanted as much as he could get. He looked up at that tree and shouted, "Hey Tree! Give me a great big, huge petal full of stew! And make it snappy!"

Well, the tree did just that. **A huge petal full of hot stew dropped down from the top of the tree full speed and crashed right on Spider's back.**

Splat! Spider fell flat on the ground.

Rabbit pulled Spider out from under the petal and helped him back home. **Rabbit stopped by Spider's house every day after that** and shared a little stew until Spider was well.

Spider finally left his bed, but he no longer walked with those straight long legs **Now he walked with crooked legs, just as he does today.**

Rain fell and the drought passed, and that strange stew tree disappeared, never to be seen again.

The End

Storytelling Tips (All Ages)

The story as presented here is a simple way to start. As you become more accustomed to using your hands while telling the tale, you can add more moves that will further engage the listeners. Here are a few suggestions:

- At the beginning of the story when telling of the drought and Spider just staying home, be specific about how Spider responds to the situation. Say, "Spider went to bed." Then make a bed with the flat of your hand and put Spider on the bed. This furthers the children's engagement because it gives them more to do with their hands. Then introduce Rabbit.

- When Rabbit discovers the tree, suggest some ways she tries to reach the petals. Have her try to jump up, but she realizes the petals are too high to reach. Have her try to climb the tree, but the trunk is too slippery. For this idea, use one arm as the tree trunk and your other hand as the rabbit trying to climb. When these attempts don't work, she sings.

- Instead of describing the falling petal as "down, down, down" use sounds to accompany the gesture of the falling petal. Sounds that are not words are common in African storytelling and are very effective here. The sound is another invitation to the listener to join in and help tell the tale.

- When Rabbit returns to the wall, instead of narration, say it rhythmically as you hop your rabbit along, "Hoppity-Hoppity-Hoppity-Hop, Hoppity-Hoppity-Hoppity-Hop, Hoppity-Hoppity-Hoppity-Hop." Then "Up [Pause] onto the wall and [Pause] over the wall." The pause offers a silent invitation for the children to join you on the phrase that follows. You can use this pause technique in many circumstances.

- Each time Rabbit returns to the wall, repeat the whole sequence from the "Hoppity-Hop" to the pauses when jumping over the wall. Likewise, each time have her sing the whole song. Then the petal floats down again, she thanks the tree again and takes a little taste once more. The repetition supports the children joining in and learning the story. Then Rabbit runs into Spider.

These are not necessary additions, just ideas for you to consider. Use what is fun for you and your listener-participants.

Activity: Telling the Story with Only Gestures (All Ages)

This tale can be told with just the finger play. It delights the children that the story makes sense even without the words.

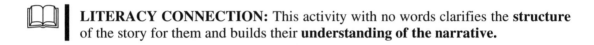

LITERACY CONNECTION: This activity with no words clarifies the **structure** of the story for them and builds their **understanding of the narrative.**

Activity: Playing the Splat Game (Pre-K–Grade 1)

After joining in on the finger play, the children can explore Spider's transformation with their whole bodies. The story becomes more vibrant to the children when they physically explore the characters. In "The Splat Game," the children sit in a line on one side of the space looking across the space. Sit in the middle of the space with your side to the children. Each child has a turn moving across the floor as a *straight-legged* spider. When a child gets in front of you, call out "Wham!" and the child splats to the ground. Then the child continues across the floor as a *crooked-legged* spider. When the spider gets to the other side, he or she sits, facing the children who have not had a turn. You can point out that there are many ways to be a long-legged spider. The children can stand up or go on hands and feet or on hands and feet with their backs facing the ground. The exploration of animal movements makes the enactment of entire stories even more exciting. This exploration is good preparation for acting out the third story in this chapter "Spider's Stew Cap."

LITERACY CONNECTION: Physically portraying the character of Spider helps with the visualization of the character when they hear other stories of the trickster spider and builds story and **narrative understanding.**

Storytelling Tips for Child Storytellers (Grades 2–4)

Children enjoy telling this story to others. They can take it home to their families and tell it there. They can tell it to younger children and to other friends. Before they do, you will want to share the story several times. Then they may think that they are ready to tell it, but you want to be sure that they have considered solutions for places they might get lost or forget. It can be demoralizing to begin telling a story only to get lost in the middle. For instance, the boys and girls may all enthusiastically chant the rabbit's song with you but later, at home by themselves, they may no longer remember the words. It is important to anticipate this possibility and discuss it with the boys and girls before it happens.

 LITERACY CONNNECTION: The examination and discussion of possible story-telling problems, besides alleviating nervousness, sets the stage for exploring the story and what is essential to the tale, and builds **narrative skills.**

It is very helpful for young readers to develop the skill of noting the basic plot elements in a story. It serves them throughout their educational career to sort out the significant parts of any text. Here's a possible dialogue:

Bill: Let's talk about telling the story at home. Let's think about what needs to be in the story for it to make sense. Do you need to say that Spider has long straight legs at the beginning?

Children: Yes!

Bill: Why?

Children: So the listener knows that spider is like that and then the ending makes sense.

Bill: What if you forget?

Children: Well, you can say you forgot and add it.

Bill: That's a great idea. It's not terrible to say you forgot. Any other ideas?

Children: You could add it later.

Bill: That's possible too. Here's another question. You know how you can sing along with a song on a CD or on the radio and you think you really know it? Then when you try to sing it by yourself, you can't remember all the words? [Students nod] Well, you've been singing the rabbit's song. What if you can't remember it when you start to tell it at home or to a friend? Should you just stop in the middle?

Children: No; you should keep telling it.

Bill: How?

Children: Make up your own song!

Bill: That would work. Any other ideas?

Children: You could just say she sings a song. Or you could sing a different song. Or …

This dialogue engages the children with the story and their relationship to it. It is better not to analyze every part of the story because the children will lose interest. You want to keep their excitement about telling the story and not turn it into a chore. For each story that the students are going to retell, find *one* or *two* spots to discuss. The skills will accumulate throughout the year. Allow these skills to develop naturally following the energy of the children.

Following the Crooked Legged Spider story, it's fun to share this one. In fact, spider can crawl right out of his bed with crooked legs and keep walking until he overhears the birds talking in this tale. For this story, ideas for including the children are within the text of the tale.

Spider at Hawk's Feast

Crooked Legged Spider went walking one day looking for food. He stopped when he heard the excited birds up in the trees.

"Chirp-chirp!"

"Tweet-tweet!"

Spider understood bird talk, and what he heard was that Hawk was planning a big feast in her nest for all the birds. Hawk was known for being an amazing cook. Hearing the birds talk about the feast made Spider even hungrier. He called up to the birds,

"Can I go? Can I go?"

The birds looked down at Spider and shook their heads,

"Sorry, Spider, but this party is just for the birds. We're afraid you can't go."

Spider looked up at the birds and thought about Hawk's feast and asked again,

"Can I go? Can I go?"

The birds replied,

"No, Spider, you can't go. We already told you. This is a party for the birds. You are a spider."

And what did Spider say? [By making this a question, you invite your listeners to respond.]

"Can I go? Can I go?"

The birds shook their heads and replied,

"We already told you. The party is for the birds. You can't go!"

And Spider?

"Can I go? Can I go?"

The birds were getting impatient and said,

"No, Spider, you may not go. Besides the party is in Hawk's nest at the top of the tallest tree. So even if you *could* go, you couldn't go. It's too far away. And we've got to get going ourselves."

Before they could fly off, the quick thinking Spider called out,

"Wait a minute. Wait a minute. I just got a great [PAUSE] "Spider Idea"! If I can fly, can I go to Hawk's feast?"

The birds all laughed and then answered,

"Ok, Spider. If you can fly you can go with us. Come on now. We've got to go."

Spider smiled and remarked,

"So you don't think I can fly, eh? Watch this!"

Spider climbed up a little bush and ran off a branch. He waved his eight legs as fast as he could. Do you think he could fly? Nope. He came crashing down. The birds started to fly off again. Spider called out,

"Wait a minute. Wait a minute. I just got a great [PAUSE—a silent invitation for the listeners to join you and say] "Spider Idea"! Will each of you give me one feather?"

The birds agreed, and each pulled out and dropped a feather. Red, blue, white and orange, gray and pink and black feathers all came floating down, down, down to the ground in front of Spider. He grabbed one in each of his eight hands and climbed up the bush again and once again ran off the branch waving the eight feathers. But did he fly? Nope. He stayed afloat for just a moment and then came crashing down. The birds said goodbye, but before they had left their trees, Spider called out again,

"Wait a minute. Wait a minute. I just got a great [PAUSE] "Spider Idea"!" The birds stopped. Spider went over to a nearby tree where the sticky sap was running down the trunk. He rubbed the sticky goop all over his body. Then he ran and jumped into the pile of feathers and rolled around.

He stood up. Spider was covered with feathers. He looked like a feather ball. The birds watched as Spider once again climbed the little bush and ran off the branch. This time he waved his eight legs and shook his whole body, and suddenly, with a little breeze beneath him, he was up in the air! He was flying and the birds led the way as Spider zigzagged through the air up towards Hawk's nest.

Spider landed on the side of Hawk's nest and joined the circle of birds. The food filled the center of the nest. Spider was ready to eat, but the birds insisted on him waiting for Hawk's arrival. Soon they could hear her winging her way to the nest, and moments later she landed. She looked pleased with all her company. She said, "Welcome all my friends." And then she began greeting her guests one at a time, "Hello there, Flamingo. Welcome, Crow. Nice to see you, Pely. Uh ...." She was staring at Spider.

"I don't think I've met you before. What is your name?"

Spider began,

"My name is Sp-"

Then he realized if he said "Spider," he would be asked to leave because this was a party for the birds. He looked around,

"My name is Flam—[muttered to himself] no, she'll never believe I'm a flamingo."

He looked around,

"My name is Cr— no, she'll never believe I'm a crow. My name is Peli—no, she'll never think I'm a pelican."

Spider looked at all the birds. He was getting frantic.

"Everyone's here already. Everyone."

Then he stopped. Spider smiled. He had a great [PAUSE] "Spider Idea." He announced,

"My name is Everyone."

"What?" asked Hawk.

"Yes, that's it," said Spider, "My name is Everyone."

Hawk shrugged and said,

"All right. Well, welcome. Now it's time for everyone to eat."

Spider stood up and announced, "Did you hear that? Hawk just said, 'It is time for *everyone* to eat.' I am Everyone. It's time for me to eat!"

With that Spider jumped into the middle of the nest and ate up all the food.

And that's the story of the day Spider tricked Hawk and ate up all of her feast.

The End

Activity: Adding an Ending (All Ages)

After having heard the crooked-legged spider story and then "Spider at Hawk's Feast," the boys and girls will be bursting with their own story ideas. You can tap this energy with a question:

"What do you think the birds did after Spider ate all the food?"

This is a nonsequential story game. Students give their own ideas to the same question. At another session, you might want to start with one of the answers and use it as a sequential story in which each student adds to what the one preceding has offered.

A Note about Questions: For years I asked the boys and girls this question, "What do you think the birds did to Spider after he ate all their food?" It seems like a perfectly reasonable question, but it aimed the children toward thinking of the birds doing something *to* Spider. When the question was changed to "What do you think the birds did after Spider ate all the feast?" without the "to Spider" in the question, there was a much wider range of imaginative responses. With this new question, many children suggest that the birds solve the problem for themselves and do nothing to Spider. Still others suggest that Spider is not allowed to come the next time. More than one child has suggested that the birds went to the stew tree described in the Crooked-Legged Spider story and got their meal there.

The Traditional Ending: The story is traditionally told that the birds threw Spider from the nest. When he landed, he went and hid. This is why you still find spiders hiding in the corners of your house. The version presented here just ends the traditional story early.

The Skeleton for "Spider at Hawk's Feast"

1. Spider goes for a walk.

2. Spider hears birds talking.

3. The birds are going to Hawk's feast!

4. Spider says, "Can I go?"

5. Birds say, "No, it's for the birds, and it's too far away."

6. Spider asks, "If I can fly, can I go?"

7. Birds say, "Yes."

8. Spider tries flying. No luck.

9. Spider gets feathers from birds and waves them. No luck.

10. Spider puts sap on his body and rolls in feathers.

11. When he jumps off a branch, he "flies."

12. He goes to Hawk's nest.

13. Hawk welcomes the birds and asks Spider's name because she does not recognize what bird he is.

14. Spider is worried. He thinks of different birds, but finally answers, "My name is Everyone!"

15. Hawk invites everyone to eat.

16. Spider is Everyone and thus eats all the food!

The End

From *Stories in Action: Interactive Tales and Learning Activities to Promote Early Literacy* by Bill Gordh. Westport, CT: Libraries Unlimited. Copyright © 2006.

After the children have heard Spider's adventure with the stew tree and Hawk's feast, they will delight in this tale of young Spider as Grandma's special helper for her feast for all the spiders. There are many places in this story to involve the children as active listeners, and it is also a wonderful story for them to act out.

Spider's Stew Cap

Every year, just as Hawk cooked a feast for all the birds, Grandma Spider made a big stew and invited all the spiders to join her. Each year she invited one of the grandchildren to come early and help her prepare for the guests. This year you can guess who it was. Little Spider! Yep, our same spider when he was little. He was so excited that he woke up extra early and went running out the door without even eating his breakfast. His mama called out,

"You better eat your breakfast!"

Little Spider called back, "No time for that. I've got to go help Grandma!"

His papa called out, "You better eat your breakfast!"

Spider kept running and called back, "No time. I've got to get to Grandma's."

He ran and ran, all the way to Grandma's. When he got there, he was panting. He knocked on the door. Grandma opened the door and smiled.

"Come in, Little Spider. I'm pleased that you're here. There is a lot to do!"

Little Spider walked in. He smelled stew! That was strange. He looked around and saw the stew boiling away in a big pot. Spider was upset,

"Grandma, you already made the stew. I thought I was going to be your special helper today."

Grandma smiled, "You are my special helper today. The stew gets better the longer it cooks, so I got up extra early and got the stew on its way. But don't worry, Little Spider. There is still plenty to do."

Spider looked at the stew and took a big whiff.

"That stew smells delicious already, Grandma!"

Grandma Spider nodded and smiled, "Well, it will only get better and that stew is for everyone when we're all together."

Spider looked at Grandma, "I know that Grandma. I'm not going to eat the stew until we're all together, right?"

"Right," said Grandma, "But just so you're not tempted, let's go outside to the garden. You can pick lettuce and I'll gather carrots and cucumbers for our salad."

Spider and his grandmother walked out to the garden and she gave him a basket for the lettuce. Then she went over a little hill to the spot the carrots and cucumbers were growing.

Spider began:

Pulling up lettuce

Putting it in the basket

Pulling up lettuce

Putting it in the basket

Pulling up lettuce

Putting it in the basket

While he was working the stew boiled and bubbled. The smell-filled steam escaped from the pot, drifted out the window, across the garden and up Little Spider's nose. It made his tummy rumble. It sounded like it was saying, "Feed me; feed me!"

Spider looked down at his hungry tummy and shouted, "Quiet tummy. Quiet tummy!"

His grandmother heard him and called, "What did you say, Little Spider?"

He didn't know what to say. He called back, "Nothing, Grandma. It's all right. It's all right."

"OK," she said. "Get back to work."

And so he did:

Pulling up lettuce

Putting it in the basket

Pulling up lettuce

Putting it in the basket

Pulling up lettuce

Putting it in the basket

The steam moved from the pot through the window and once again up Spider's nose. His tummy rumbled even louder, "Feed me; feed me!"

Spider shouted at his tummy, "Quiet tummy. Quiet tummy!"

His grandmother called, "What did you say Little Spider?"

He called back, "Nothing, Grandma. It's all right. It's all right."

"OK," she said. "Get back to work."

So he did

Pulling up lettuce

Putting it in the basket

Pulling up lettuce

Putting it in the basket

Pulling up lettuce

Putting it in the basket

The steam moved through the window and up Spider's nose. His tummy rumbled even louder, "Feed me; feed me!"

Spider shouted, "Quiet tummy. Quiet tummy!"

His grandmother called, "What did you say Little Spider?"

He called back, "Nothing, Grandma. It's all right. It's all right."

"OK," she said. "Get back to work."

It was a hot morning, and Spider wiped the sweat from his brow. He called, "Grandma, may I go inside and get a drink of water? It's really hot."

She replied, "OK, but do NOT taste the stew!"

Spider answered, "Don't worry, Grandma I'm not going to taste the stew."

Little Spider went inside and got a drink of water. He started to leave, but the stew smelled even better inside and his tummy went wild!

"Feed me! Feed me!"

Little Spider pleaded with his tummy, "Quiet tummy, quiet tummy!"

He looked at the stew. There was plenty in that big pot. He thought, "You know; there is so much stew. It's probably OK if I taste just a little."

He looked around and saw a bowl. He shook his head, "No, I can't use that. Grandma might see it."

He scratched his head. He was wearing a cap. The cap gave him a great "Spider Idea"!

"I can use my cap for a bowl!"

And he dipped his cap into the hot stew and took a taste. It was delicious, and he slurped it up. He dipped his cap in again. He was ready to eat some more when the door opened. Standing in the doorway was his Grandma and with her the rest of the guests, his mother and father, brothers and sisters and all of the cousins!

Spider quickly took the stew-filled cap and put it back on his head! The stew was hot!!!! Spider started jumping up and down yelping. His cousins thought he was dancing and everyone began clapping and shouting, "Dance it, Spider, Dance it!"

He kept jumping around until a bit of carrot slipped out of his cap and slid down his nose. He stopped dancing. Grandma walked over and pulled his cap off his head. The leftover stew plopped on the ground. Before he could say a thing, one of his sisters called out, "Little Spider, you're bald!"

Little Spider ran over to the mirror and looked. Not one hair was left on his head. Ever since that day, spiders have bald heads, but every time they have a party, they always ask Little Spider to do his fabulous cap dance again.

The End

Activity: Acting out the Story (All Ages)

 **LITERACY CONNECTION:** Acting out stories helps children internalize the **structure** of the tale and builds **comprehension skills** as well as confidence.

Although generally this book suggests the acting out of stories for Pre-K to Grade 1, this story works well with any age. It can become a wonderful performance piece for a third- or fourth-grade class using one or more narrators to tell the story. As always, name the characters and point to positions around the open space. Ask if there are any additional characters.

(*Note:* This is the story that clued me in on the importance of asking if there were any characters I had not named that they wished to portray. See Introduction.) As always, remind everyone of the three rules for acting out stories:

1. Listen to the Storyteller.

2. Be safe!

3. Have fun!

Some additional tips for acting out this story:

- If you have a few Grandmas or Grandpas, let them have some fun making the stew, naming the vegetables and chopping them up and stirring the stew. (See Stew Making game following "The Big Turnip" story in Chapter 13.)

- If you choose to use the Little Spider and Grandma dialogue when they are in the garden, you will discover that often the children remember the lines and say them, but be prepared to provide the dialogue if they don't.

Activity: Adding an Ending (Grades 2–4)

If your students enjoyed adding endings to the "Hawk's Feast" story, you can use this story in a similar way. Retell the story as it is printed above and STOP the story at the point when Spider is holding the cap full of stew and the relatives have just opened the door. Then ask the children, "What do you think Spider did?"

Since you know the ending, you may think it is the only possible one. Well, you're in for a surprise—the children are likely to suggest many, many different endings, endings that reflect their understanding of the story, their own beliefs about what should happen when someone gets caught, their cultural attitudes towards the behavior described, and so on. It is fascinating. Sometimes the children will ask what the "real" ending is. Some people feel that if the children have supplied endings, you should leave it at that and not tell the ending. They suggest that then the children compare their endings to the "real" ending and become more concerned with whether they were right or not, which is clearly not the point. Others feel that you can celebrate the endings the children give and tell the traditional ending as well. It is up to you, but if you do tell the "real" ending, follow it with a discussion of the many different endings and what everyone noticed about them. They may like their own endings better. All in all, what is important is that they are not trying to guess the ending but rather to contribute their own.

 LITERACY CONNECTION: Narrative skills: Original story endings grow from the children's understanding of the characters and events in the story and how they can use their own imagination in relation to these elements.

The Skeleton for "Spider's Stew Cap"

1. Grandma Spider is making stew.

2. Little Spider goes to help.

3. Stew smells good, so Grandma leads Spider to the garden.

4. The stew is for the whole family.

5. The smell of the stew makes Little Spider hungry.

6. Little Spider goes back inside.

7. The stew smells really good.

8. Little Spider decides to take a taste but doesn't know what to use for a bowl.

9. Little Spider uses his cap and dips it in the stew.

10. The family comes in.

11. Little Spider puts his stew-filled cap back on his head.

12. The hot stew makes him dance around.

13. They think he's dancing but then—

14. He is discovered!

15. Grandma pulls off his cap.

16. Spider has a bald head.

The End

From *Stories in Action: Interactive Tales and Learning Activities to Promote Early Literacy* by Bill Gordh. Westport, CT: Libraries Unlimited. Copyright © 2006.

Three Spider Stories: Notes on Three Ways of Working

There are so many exciting Spider stories that it was hard to choose which ones to share in this book. I chose the first three, however, because they offer three approaches that you can use with other stories.

1. **Finger Play:** The first is the finger play that gets the stationary listeners physically involved with the structure and language of the story.

2. **Add an Ending**: The second provides children with a dynamic story to which they are eager to contribute endings.

3. **Act it Out:** The third is perfect for acting out. The children learn the structure of the tale from the inside out, internalizing the structure of the story by being part of the story itself.

 LITERACY CONNECTION: As literacy builders these methods of finger play, adding an ending and acting the story out work hand in hand to engage the children in meaningful language-rich activities building **vocabulary** awareness and **narrative skills.**

We conclude our chapter with a final spider story, a simple one that is easy to tell. It's perfect when you want a quick, fun, and meaningful story to share. This story is also told in the Caribbean where many of the Spider tales traveled and slowly gained their own distinctive Caribbean flavor. We have stayed with the West African tales for this book.

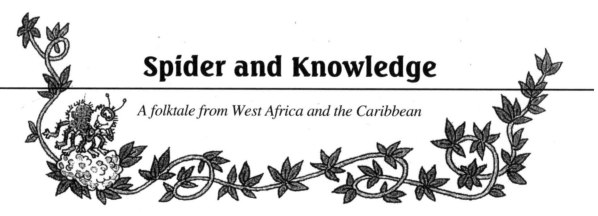

Spider and Knowledge

A folktale from West Africa and the Caribbean

Spider thought he knew everything! He looked around and said, "I am the smartest in the whole world! No one is as smart as I am. In fact, I think I'll gather up the few things I don't know, and then I'll have all the knowledge in the world!" He smiled at this thought.

Spider went to work. He took a big gourd, shaped **kind of like a pumpkin, hollowed it out,** and fixed it up with a stopper. Then he started gathering knowledge.
A little here—stuff it into the gourd.
A little there—stuff it into the gourd.
Everywhere he went, he gathered more knowledge and stuffed it into his gourd.

Finally the gourd was very full. Spider smiled. He now had all the knowledge in the world! He pushed the stopper into the gourd and looked around for a place to hide his treasure. He was not going to share it with anyone.

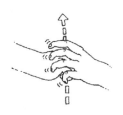

When he saw a palm tree, he knew he had found the perfect hiding place. He was so smart! **He took hold of the gourd, held it close to his belly and started climbing.** It was tricky going. Spider kept slipping with that gourd between him and the tree.

He heard some laughter from the bottom of the tree. He looked down. There were two of his children, a son and a daughter. He said, "What are you laughing about?"

They called back, "Carry the gourd on your back! It will be a lot easier."

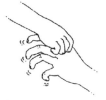

Spider heard what they said and realized they were right. **He flipped the gourd over his shoulder and climbed easily up the rest of the tree.**

When he got to the top, he realized he had not gathered all the knowledge, for his very own children knew something he didn't know. This made him so angry that **he flung the gourd down to the ground.**

The gourd smashed into thousands of pieces, and knowledge scattered across the world.

That's why we all know something.

The End

There are a number of very good picture books of Spider trickster tales. Here are a few to enjoy sharing with your boys and girls.

Thematic Picture Book Suggestions

 LITERACY CONNECTION: Print awareness and **print motivation.** Children love these West African spider tales and joining in on the activities presented in this chapter. Introducing some books starring Anansi will only further their engagement with the trickster spider. Even very young children who cannot read will enjoy looking at and handling these books.

Cabral, Len, and David Diaz (illustrator). *Anansi's Narrow Waist: An African Folk Tale.* GoodYear Books, 1994.

Kimmel, Eric, and Janet Stevens. *Anansi Goes Fishing.* Holiday House (reprint ed.), 1993.

Kimmel, Eric, and Janet Stevens. *Anansi and the Magic Stick.* Holiday House, 2002.

McDermott, Gerald. *Anansi the Spider: A Tale from the Ashanti.* Henry Holt, 1987.

Part Three

Exploring Cultures through Stories

Chapter 8
Learning about Mexican Culture through Folktales

The finger play that opens this chapter of Mexican tales features three vegetables common in Mexican cooking: the onion, the tomato, and the chili pepper. However, in this tale they don't wind up in a pot, they eat cherries! This crazy story gets children excited to learn more about Mexican culture.

Finger Play Warm-Up

After doing the usual finger warm-up, you might ask some of the children to offer a move that everyone will copy. Having children lead the warm-up will support their own storytelling because it makes them more aware of how their fingers are moving and what they might signify. When everyone is settled, you can begin this story.

The Wild Cherry Tree

A Folktale from Mexico

Once there was a little old man and a little old woman **and they were sitting at the table in their house.**

On the table was **a tomato,**

an onion,

and a chili pepper.

The little old man and the little old woman
needed some water.

**So the tomato rolled off the table
and headed toward the river to fetch some.**

On the way, the tomato saw the cherry tree.
Oooh! Those cherries looked good!

**The tomato climbed up into the cherry tree
and started eating cherries.**

The little old man and the little old woman
sat at their table and waited for the tomato to
return. They waited and waited and waited.

They decided to send the onion.

**The onion rolled off the table
and headed toward the river to get some water.**

On the way, the onion saw the cherry tree.
Oooh! Those cherries looked good!

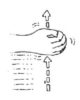

**The onion climbed up into the cherry tree
and started eating cherries.**

The little old man and the little old woman
sat at their table and waited for the onion.
They waited and waited and waited.

They decided to send the chili pepper.

The chili pepper jumped off the table
and headed toward the river to get some water.

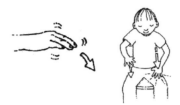

On the way, the chili pepper saw the cherry tree.
Oooh! Those cherries looked good!

**The chili pepper climbed up into the cherry
tree and started eating cherries.**

The little old man and the little old woman
sat at their table and waited. They waited and
waited and waited. They looked at each other, got
up, **and headed for the river.**

On the way, they saw the cherry tree.
Oooh! Those cherries looked good!

The little old man and the little old woman
 climbed up into the cherry tree
and started eating cherries.

There they were—the little old man, the little old
woman, the tomato, the onion, and the chili pepper—
all up in the tree, **eating cherries!**

It so happened that **it was raining up** in the mountains,
and this caused the river to flood.

The river's waters rose higher and higher and higher.

The flooding river pulled the tree right out of the ground and **carried it and all its passengers downstream into the Gulf of Mexico.**

The little old man and the little old woman and the tomato and the onion and the chili pepper **swam to shore** and walked back home.

The little old man and the little old woman **sat down at the table.**

The tomato,
the onion,
and the **chili pepper**
climbed back up onto the table.

And do you know what?

The little old man and the little old woman
still needed some water.

The End

Storytelling Tips (All Ages)

After you get used to sharing the simple version of this story, you can add to it and make the tale even more exciting to your listeners. The additions make the children more eager to tell the tale themselves. This story is good for third and fourth graders to retell, but might be a bit tricky for second graders. The tale works quite well as told above, but some or all of these additional ideas may spark your own excitement in telling the story.

- After you have said that the old man and old woman need water, it's fun to have the couple argue. The old man says, "I'm thirsty. Would you go down to the river and get some water?"

The old woman replies, "I don't want to go. You go!" The old man says, "No, you go!" Repeat this a few times and then say, "Finally the tomato said, 'Quiet, you two! I'll go get the water." The children really enjoy the tomato talking. Repeat the couple's argument for each of the vegetables. With these additions, you now have vegetables that talk, roll, climb, and eat. Who wouldn't delight in that?

- When each vegetable climbs into the tree, turn the cherry-eating action into a little chant that the boys and girls join.

  Eating up cherries and spitting out the pits

  Puh-Puh-Puh-Puh

  Eating up cherries and spitting out the pits

  Puh-Puh-Puh-Puh

- At the end of the tale have the old man say as he did at the beginning, "I'm thirsty."

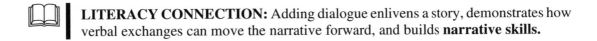 **LITERACY CONNECTION:** Adding dialogue enlivens a story, demonstrates how verbal exchanges can move the narrative forward, and builds **narrative skills.**

Activity: Acting out the Story (Pre-K–Grade 1)

This is a great story for acting out. It offers a wide range of characters that are not typical to tales. After hearing and acting out this story, the children begin considering a wider range of active characters for their own story creations. The dialogue offered in the suggested additions can be incorporated into this activity. As always, announce the characters and point to positions around the acting out space. Name the two people, the tomato, the onion, the chili pepper, and the cherry tree. You can also include the river and the storm in the mountains. When the river floods, the storm and rain children join the river and help "carry away" the tree and its occupants. If two children don't want to be the old man and old woman, tell the story with two old men or two old women. Of course you can have more than two, but everyone will agree that the story needs to have the people or it won't work. Remind everyone of the rules. This story is a little wild, so a safety reminder is in order:

1. Listen to the storyteller! ("So you know what's going on. Sometimes the story changes a bit when it is acted out, so you need to hear it all!")

2. Be safe! ("Watch out for your own body and others.")

3. Have fun!

The boys and girls will want to return to this story many times. As you get more comfortable telling the tale for acting out, you can add other details.

Activity: Adding Characters to the Tale (All Ages)

If you are using this story in the context of a unit on Mexico, you can discuss what other vegetables and cooking implements might be on the scene. The story is sometimes told with a mortar and pestle on the table. Together you can retell the tale with the added characters.

LITERACY CONNECTION: Adding characters shows the children that the **structure** of a story allows for some changes and reinforces their sense of what elements need to be constant. It also builds **narrative skills.** Adding elements specific to life in Mexico will help build the children's cultural vocabularies, increasing **phonological awareness** and building **vocabulary skills.**

"The Wild Cherry Tree" is not a "typical" Mexican tale. All too often the typical tales reinforce negative stereotypes of the culture we are trying to appreciate. It is important to include a wide range of stories when exploring any culture. The following is a favorite in Mexico and enjoyed by girls and boys everywhere because the child in the story becomes the parent's teacher.

Half a Blanket

A Tale from Mexico

Once there was a girl named Juanita. Juanita lived with her mother and father in a small house. She was a happy girl who enjoyed singing and playing, and she simply loved to listen to stories. Her favorite storyteller was her grandpa, who told her all kinds of tales: funny stories about Coyote, amazing stories about the sun and moon and stars, exciting tales of families and friends. He always had a story for Juanita and often a song, too. Juanita loved her grandpa.

When her grandmother died, Grandpa moved in with Juanita and her parents. The house was already small for the three of them. Now, with Grandpa living there too, it was crowded. Still Juanita loved it, for she got to see her grandpa every day. Every night she listened to his wonderful stories. But this new living situation was not so good for Juanita's mother and father. The house was just too small for them all to live in peace. Grandpa was in the way.

One evening Juanita heard her parents talking. They decided to move Grandpa out to the shed behind the house. They would give him a little cot and a chest of drawers and he would still eat meals with them. When Papa told him the plan, Grandpa agreed and soon he was set up in the little shack.

Things went along fine for a while. Grandpa joined them for breakfast, lunch, and supper, and Juanita visited him to listen to his stories and songs. But as the days grew colder, things changed. Grandpa did not always come for supper, and some days Juanita did not visit her grandpa. One evening after a supper without Grandpa, Juanita went to see him in his shack. She found him lying on his bed shivering with cold. He said, "Sweet Juanita, please bring your grandpa a blanket."

Juanita ran back to the house. She began searching through the closets. "What are you doing, Juanita!" asked her mother. "What's going on?" asked her father.

"I'm looking for a blanket!" she replied.

"What for?" asked her father.

"Grandpa is cold!" answered Juanita. Her father walked to the bedroom closet and got out a blanket. "Here, Juanita, take this to Grandpa." Juanita took the blanket, thought for a moment and then asked, "Will you cut it in half, please?"

Juanita's father stared at her, "Cut it in half?! What are you talking about? It's a good blanket. I'm not going to cut it in half!" Juanita looked up at her father, "But Papa, I need you to cut it in half, so that I can give half to grandpa now and save the other half-blanket for you when you are old. I don't want you to ever be cold."

When he heard his daughter's words, tears filled his eyes. "Juanita," Papa said, "Oh, Juanita, Juanita, thank you. You have reminded me of what is really important in life. Come, let's go get Grandpa and bring him home. What do you say?"

Juanita said, "Yes! Let's go, Papa!" and they went out and brought Grandpa back into their home. And in the house is where he stayed.

Now, even with Grandpa and all his stories and songs, the little house does not seem crowded at all. It feels just right!

The End

Activity: Sharing Stories about Grandparents (All Ages)

This story with loads of heart feels like it could be a true story. This kind of story inspires very different story ideas than a tale like "The Wild Cherry Tree." This story calls forth personal stories and offers a framework for children to share their own grandparent tales. Not everyone will have a grandparent story to share, so you should follow the lead of the upraised hands.

 **LITERACY CONNECTION:** Telling personal stories in the context of a class builds **narrative skills** and makes the children aware of how they often tell stories without thinking about it.

The Skeleton for "Half a Blanket"

1. Juanita lives with mother and father in a small house.

2. Juanita visits her grandfather, who tells her stories.

3. Grandmother dies and Grandpa moves into Juanita's house.

4. The house feels very crowded.

5. They move Grandpa into shack behind the house.

6. Juanita still visits. Grandpa eats with the family.

7. Time goes by.

8. They see Grandpa less and less.

9. Juanita visits Grandpa.

10. He is cold and asks for a blanket.

11. Juanita runs inside to find blanket.

12. Juanita opens closet and Papa helps find a blanket.

13. Juanita asks for scissors.

14. What for?

15. She says she wants half for Grandpa and half for Papa so that when he gets old, he won't be cold.

16. They bring Grandpa back into the house.

17. The house doesn't seem so crowded as stories and songs fill their hearts.

The End

From *Stories in Action: Interactive Tales and Learning Activities to Promote Early Literacy* by Bill Gordh. Westport, CT: Libraries Unlimited. Copyright © 2006.

Stories of the trickster Coyote have been told for years by indigenous North Americans from Mexico all the way up to Western Canada. These tales predate the Spanish presence and provide the listeners a marvelous character to add to their appreciation of Mexico and pre-European America. There are many great Coyote tales, and you might want to create a unit exploring just Coyote as we did in the previous chapter with the trickster Spider.

Coyote's Tail

Coyote was out on the prairie. His ears suddenly perked up. From across the plains he heard, "Ruff-ruff-ruff-ruff." He looked with his keen eyes. He saw a cloud of dust. The cloud was coming his way. His ears perked up again. The sound was louder, "Ruff, ruff, ruff, ruff." He looked again. Looked like dogs! He took a sniff: smelled like dogs! "P-U!" He remembered something: "I think those are the same big dogs that were sleeping yesterday when I borrowed some of their food. They are probably mad—at me!" He listened. The barks were getting louder, "Ruff, ruff, ruff!" He looked: the cloud was getting closer. He sniffed, "P-U!" He looked at his legs, "OK, legs, time to get to work for old Coyote." And Coyote's legs took off and carried Coyote over the hills, across the arroyos, faster than fast. He listened, "Ruff, ruff, ruff!" He looked back—Sharp teeth! He sniffed, "P-U!!" He ran. Then he spotted a hole. "OK, legs," he cried, "Jump me into that hole!"

In a flash Coyote, was in the hole. The hole was just the right size for Coyote, but the opening was too small for the dogs to follow him in. Coyote was safe in the hole with the angry dogs barking outside. Coyote howled with laughter. After a while the dogs stopped barking and just lay down to wait. Coyote was in the hole with nothing to do! He decided to have a little chat. He looked around in the hole. Dirt! "I'm not going to talk to dirt!" said Coyote. He looked around some more. Rocks! "I'm not talking to rocks!" He looked around some more—a worm! "I'm not talking to a worm!" He looked around. Then he got an idea. He said, "I know; I'll talk to myself! Who could be better than me to talk to? I'll start with my ears." And Coyote spoke to his ears, "Ears. Ears, what did you do for me today?" Coyote's ears answered, "What did we do? We were the ones who heard that barking from far, far away. We warned you!"

Coyote smiled, "That's right, ears. You did a great job and

You will *be*

Part of *me*

FOREVER!"

Coyote spoke to his eyes next, "Eyes, eyes, what did you do for me today?"

The eyes answered, "What did we do? We spotted those dogs when they were just a cloud of dust!" Coyote smiled, "That's right, eyes. You did a great job and

You will *be*

Part of *me*

FOREVER!"

After his eyes Coyote spoke to his nose, "Nose, nose what did you do for me today?" Nose replied, "Are you kidding? I had to smell those smelly dogs! P-U!!" Coyote nodded again and smiled, "That's right, nose. You did a great job and

You will *be*

Part of *me*

FOREVER!"

Now Coyote looked at his four legs and asked them the same question, "Legs, what did you do for me today?" Coyote's legs answered, "What did we do? We ran, ran, ran and then leaped into this hole. That's what we did." Coyote smiled, "That's right, legs. You did a great job and

You will *be*

Part of *me*

FOREVER!"

Coyote noticed his tail. He considered not even asking his tail, stuck way back there at the end of his body, but he had nothing else to do. So he asked in a nasty, sarcastic voice, "And what did you do, Tail? Probably just slowed me down, right?" Well, Tail had not slowed Coyote down and until this moment had been proud of Coyote's escape. But now Tail's feelings were hurt, so Tail replied, "That's right, Coyote; I slowed you down. I also wagged and waved at those dogs saying 'Come on, dogs! Bite Coyote, bite Coyote!' "

Coyote was shocked and amazed. He said to his tail, "I should have known you'd be like that. Well, you do not deserve to be part of the great Coyote's body and

You shall NOT be

Part of me

Ever again!"

So Tail you just leave. Go on! Get out of here. I don't want you anymore!" But Tail did not move. Coyote spoke louder and it woke up the dogs, "I said,

You shall NOT be

Part of me

Ever again!"

Now get out of this hole!" The dogs listened at the opening of the hole. Inside the hole Tail still did not move. Coyote was really angry now! "I said, 'Get out of this hole!' Still not moving, eh? OK, then I'll just push you out!' " So Coyote backed his own tail out of the hole!
OW-ooooooooooooo!

The End

Acting out the Story (Pre-K–Grade 1)

This is an unusual story to act out, but after acting out "The Wild Cherry Tree," the children will prove to you that they can act out anything. Having different children play the various body parts is great fun, and in your retelling you can give each a chance to demonstrate what she or he can do.

Activity: Creating Dialogue with Body Parts as Characters (All Ages)

The notion of different body parts conversing is an invitation for imaginative thinking. You can tap into this thinking by suggesting circumstances for which the children offer body part dialog. Here are a few examples:

- Say to children: "You have been hiking through the woods. You've traveled through thick underbrush and walked on bare forest floor beneath tall pines. You've stomped through deep mud and now you sit down on a log. What do your feet say?"

- You just finished trick-or-treating but have not eaten one piece of candy. What does your stomach say?

- You are a tightrope walker in the circus one hundred feet above the crowd. What do your eyes say?

There are endless variations, and after you suggest a few, let the children create scenarios. It gets them to place their bodies in different circumstances and create little stories all in a game-like setting.

 LITERACY CONNECTION: Creating dialogue supports the understanding of how it works in the context of story to further the action. It also strengthens **narrative skills.**

The Skeleton for "Coyote's Tail"

1. Coyote is out on the plain. He listens.

2. Dogs.

3. Coyote looks. Dogs.

4. Coyote smells. Dogs.

5. They are coming after him!

6. Coyote runs.

7. Dogs chase him.

8. He looks, listens, smells, and runs.

9. He jumps in a hole too small for the dogs to follow him.

10. The dogs wait outside.

11. Coyote talks to himself—talking to his various body parts.

12. He asks each what they did for him. Ears. Eyes. Nose. Legs.

13. Each tells how it helped him.

14. Coyote looks at Tail and complains that it slowed him down.

15. Tail did not slow him down but is mad and says it did.

16. Coyote tells Tail to leave.

17. Tail does not leave.

18. Coyote backs tail out of hole.

19. The dogs are waiting.

The End

From *Stories in Action: Interactive Tales and Learning Activities to Promote Early Literacy*
by Bill Gordh. Westport, CT: Libraries Unlimited. Copyright © 2006.

This chapter offers just a sampling of Mexican Folktales. There are many, many more that you will enjoy using and many of the activities described in this chapter can be applied to the other tales you discover. Following are some picture books of Mexican tales you'll enjoy sharing. You will also find the name of some good collections that contain Mexican Tales in the reference page at the end of the book.

Thematic Picture Book Suggestions

 LITERACY CONNECTION: Picture books offer children a rich addition to this exploration of Mexican culture. The stories in this chapter increase **print motivation** and energize the children to find more tales that enrich their understanding. **Offering children a selection of books to peruse or read increases print awareness, showing them the connection between story and print.**

Aardema, Verna, and Petra Mathers. *Borreguita and the Coyote*. Dragonfly Books (reprint ed.), 1998.

Cruz Martinez, Alejandro, and Fernando Olivera. *The Woman Who Outshone The Sun/La mujer que brillaba aún más que el sol* (English/Spanish bilingual). Sagebrush, 1999.

McDermott, Gerald. *Musicians of the Sun*. Simon & Schuster Children's Publishing, 1997.

Mike, Jan. *Opossum and the Great Firemaker: A Mexican Legend*. Sagebrush, 2001.

Chapter 9
Learning about the Brazilian Amazon through Folktales

Regional folktales always enrich the understanding of a particular place in the world. Although many folktales have traveled all around the world and their basic structures stay the same, the details often change to reflect the culture of the place where they are told. They change to include the geography, the names, the animals, and the beliefs of the people retelling the tales. Geographically specific animals that appear in the tales provide an added dimension to the story and often entice children to learn more about a place or culture. In this chapter, we travel to the Amazon region of South America.

Finger Play Warm-Up

Following the warm-up but before starting the story, show your monkeys playing around by tumbling your slightly closed fists around in front of you while making monkey sounds. Invite the listeners to join you.

The Tomorrow Monkeys

A Folktale from Brazil

This is a story from Brazil about some little monkeys who play along the river, the Rio Negro. **They play and play and play all day** beneath the warm sun and the blue skies.

And when the sun goes down,
the monkeys climb up the tall palm trees,
and the clouds roll in,
and the rain starts falling,
and the wind begins to blow.
It gets cold and soon **those monkeys are shivering, shivering.**

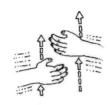

In the middle of the night,
the papa monkeys cry out,
"Let's build a house tomorrow,
let's build a house tomorrow!"

And the mama monkeys shout, "Yes, let's build a house tomorrow,
Let's build a house."

And the littlest monkeys agree,
"Yeh-yeh-yeh-yeh-yeh-yeh-yeh!"

In the morning,
the sun comes up, the clouds roll away,
it's another beautiful, blue-sky day,
And the little monkeys climb down to play.

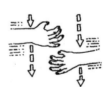

And they play and play 'til one of the monkeys scratches her
head and says, "Weren't we going to build a house today?"

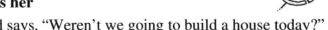

And the other monkeys say, "It's a beautiful day;

let's play, let's play. We can build the
house tomorrow."
And they play and play and play.

'Til the sun goes down,
and the monkeys climb up the tall palm trees,
and the clouds roll in,
and the rain starts falling,
and the wind blows.

It gets cold
and soon those monkeys are shivering again.

And in the middle of the night,
the papa monkeys cry out,
"Let's build a house tomorrow, let's build a house tomorrow!"

And the mama monkeys shout, "Yes, let's build a house
tomorrow,
Let's build a house."

And the littlest monkeys agree,
"Yeh-yeh-yeh-yeh-yeh-yeh-yeh!"

In the morning,
the sun comes up, the clouds roll away,
it's another beautiful, blue-sky day,
And the little monkeys climb down to play.

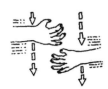

And they play and play 'til one of the monkeys scratches her head and says, "Weren't we going to build a house today?"

And the other monkeys say, "It's a beautiful day; let's play, let's play. We can build the house tomorrow." And they play and play and play.

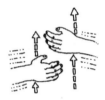

'Til the sun goes down, **and the monkeys climb their trees,**

and the clouds roll in, and the rain starts falling, and the wind blows. It gets cold and soon **those monkeys are shivering again.**

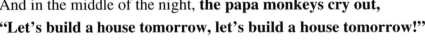

And in the middle of the night, **the papa monkeys cry out, "Let's build a house tomorrow, let's build a house tomorrow!"**

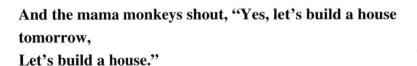

And the mama monkeys shout, "Yes, let's build a house tomorrow, Let's build a house."

And the littlest monkeys agree, "Yeh-yeh-yeh-yeh-yeh-yeh-yeh!"

In the morning,
the sun comes up, the clouds roll away,
it's another beautiful, blue-sky day,
And the little monkeys climb down to play.

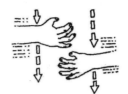

And they play and play 'til one of the monkeys scratches her head and says, "Weren't we going to build a house today?"

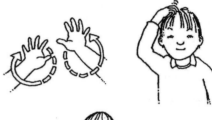

And do you think they ever build a house?

The End

Storytelling Tips (All Ages)

Having more finger play illustrations to accompany this story would make it appear confusing, and the story works well the way it is presented. However, you can add a number of gestures to make the structural sequencing of the story even clearer. In fact, after telling it a few times, you can retell the story with gestures alone. You might add these:

- When the sun goes down—*Flat hand (sun) going down from shoulder to waist*

- Monkeys climb up—Illustrated in book

- And the clouds roll in—*Roll slightly closed fist around and around forward*

- And the rain starts falling—*Up to down movement of hands with fingers wiggling*

- Monkeys shivering—see illustration

This repeats a few times, so your listeners will join you on all the movements and soon will say the words along with the gestures. The sequence of gestures will make the story easier for the students to tell on their own. When the sun comes up (in the story) and the clouds roll away, you can use the gestures just described, but reversing the motions.

 LITERACY CONNECTION: Adding gestures to the finger play clarifies the sequence of events and the repetition of the sequence and supports **narrative skills.**

Activity: Acting out the Story (Pre-K–Grade 1)

This is a great story for acting out. Everyone is a monkey! You can have the father monkeys on one side of the space, the mama monkeys on another side, and the littlest on the third side with you retelling the tale from the fourth side. Ask the children to call out the rules, "Listen to the storyteller, be safe, and have fun!" The children's positions on the sides of the open space represent their homes in the trees. Their play space is the open space in the middle. This story suggests no specific play for the monkeys, and it is fun to watch how the children-monkeys use this free-play monkey time. After some monkey play, continue with the story. If it gets a little too rowdy, go ahead and have the sun go down because that's when all the monkeys climb up into their trees.

Activity: A Variation on Acting out the Story: Building the House (Pre-K–Grade 1)

You might notice with some Pre-K and K groups that they are unhappy with the ending of this story. They want to build the house! So you can say, "Well, we know that in the story, the monkeys never build a house, but would you monkeys like to today?" If they say yes, which they probably will, you can end the story with the monkeys building a house. Depending on the time you have, you can ask various monkeys as they work about which tools they are using and what part of the house they are building. They can paint the house and tell you the colors.

 LITERACY CONNECTION: Allowing children to comment on the details of their contributions to a story as they act it out confirms their roles as story-makers, a role that gives them assurance in future encounters with story and builds **narrative skills.**

To finish the story with the newly built house, say, "And when the sun goes down, what do the monkeys do?" The children will call out, "Go in their house!" And they do. All the monkeys go into the house they just built. When the clouds roll in and the rain falls down, the monkeys are warm and dry, sleeping in their new house!

Activity: Discussing the Story (Grades 2–4)

This is a great story for the boys and girls to retell. It also is a good tale to discuss. After you have told the tale a couple of times (the first time they will be engaged with the finger play and the fun of the story), ask the students why someone would tell this story. Collect answers. Then ask if they have ever been "Tomorrow Monkeys" and to share their own stories.

 LITERACY CONNECTION: Setting up frameworks for the children's personal stories builds **narrative skills** by helping children organize their thoughts and experiences and noticing how authors do the same.

This story can also be used in conjunction with Chapter 14. It is a great example of a multicycle circle story.

The next story in our exploration of the Amazon tells of a turtle that can play the flute! Not only is it musical; it's also quite clever.

The Tricky Turtle

There was once a turtle that lived deep in the forest. Every morning when it woke up, it crawled down to the river for a drink. After its morning swallow, it pulled out a flute and played a beautiful little song that accompanied the sound of the flowing waters.

On the day of this story, a man was searching in the forest for food for his family. He had found some berries and nuts, but not enough for dinner. That's when he heard the turtle's song. He moved through the forest as quietly as he could while following the beautiful song. He had never heard a flute played so beautifully. He saw the turtle, but the turtle did not see him. The father smiled. "That turtle will make a delicious soup!" he said to himself.

He moved back into the forest away from the river. He pulled his big chopping knife out of his belt and began chopping branches and liana vines—Chop-chop-chop. Chop-chop-chop. Chop-chop-chop. He made a cage with the wood he had cut and tied it together with the vines. He carried it very quietly and sneaked up behind the turtle. He placed the cage over the top of the turtle. The turtle immediately ducked inside its shell as the man closed the cage and picked it up. He carried it all the way back through the forest until he came to the little clearing in front of his house.

He called out, "Children, children, come out! See what I have caught!" His son and daughter ran outside and peered into the cage.

"A turtle!" exclaimed the sister.

"A turtle!" exclaimed the brother.

"Yes!" said the father, "And we will have turtle soup for supper. With our loaf of bread and the soup, we will have a fine dinner."

Brother and Sister were excited, "Papa, how can we help?"

"Go and get the pot!" he replied and the two children ran into the house and brought out the big soup pot. "Now what?" they asked.

"Fill it with water!" replied Papa and Brother and Sister filled the pot with water. They looked at their father waiting to hear the next thing to do.

"Go around back and get some firewood." The children ran behind the house.

Soon they returned, but with only one stick of firewood. Papa looked at the stick and shook his head. "That will not be enough firewood," he said, "So I will go into the forest and gather more."

"What can we do?" asked Brother and Sister.

"Well," said their father, "I will give you a very important job."

"Great!" they replied. Papa looked at his two children and over at the caged turtle. "I want the two of you to watch that turtle and make sure it does not get out. It is going to be our supper!"

"But it's in a cage. Of course it won't get out," said the sister. "Well, just make sure it stays there."

"OK," said Brother.

"OK!" said Sister.

They sat down in front of the cage and looked at the turtle as their father returned to the forest to gather more firewood.

They watched the turtle. The turtle was still tucked away in its shell. The children looked away. The turtle spoke, "Hey!"

Sister looked at Brother, "Did you say that?" Brother said, "I didn't say anything."

"I said, 'Hey!'" said the turtle. They stared at the turtle that had just stuck out its head. "A talking turtle!" exclaimed both children.

"I can also play the flute!" boasted the turtle.

"That's not true!" said the brother.

"It is," said the turtle.

"Show us!" exclaimed both children.

"Well, I'd love to, but it's too crowded in here. You have to open the cage, so I can stick my head and arms out."

The brother and sister shook their heads, "No, we can't let you out. Our papa asked us to watch you and to make sure you did not get out of that cage."

The turtle looked at the sister and brother, "Oh, I don't need to get out of the cage! Just open the cage door so I can stick my head and arms out to play the flute. My body will still be in the cage."

"OK!" they said and opened the cage door. The turtle did as it promised and stayed inside the cage and began playing its flute. It was beautiful! The turtle stopped.

"Play more!" cried Sister.

"More!" begged brother.

"Well I could play some more. In fact I can even dance while I am playing." They stared at the turtle. They could not believe it. They shook their heads. The turtle continued, "It's true. I can play and dance at the same time. Of course, I can't really dance in this little cage."

Brother and Sister let the turtle out of the cage so it could show them its dance and the turtle was telling the truth! Turtle was a great dancer! The music was so wonderful and the turtle's dance was so energetic that Brother and Sister started dancing, too. They danced and danced and danced, swirling and twirling around. As they were swirling, the turtle was dancing its way toward the edge of the clearing and soon slipped into the forest. When it found a nice bushy bush, it crawled under and stopped playing. The silence stopped the dance. Brother and Sister looked around. No turtle! They looked at each other. "Oh no!" they cried.

They ran into the forest looking for the turtle. "Is that it?" they ran to see. Nope, just a big rock. "Is that it?" They ran. Another big rock. Papa would be back soon. They got an idea. They had mistaken a rock for a turtle. Maybe their father would, too. They found a rock about the size of their turtle and carried it back home. They put it in the cage and added some tall grass and leaves. Papa walked into the clearing carrying an armful of firewood. He set it down and built a fire. Soon the water was boiling.

"Everything OK?" he asked. They did not say a thing. Papa picked up the cage and opened the little door. He dumped the rock into the pot. It made a big splash. "I never saw a turtle make such a big splash," Papa said. Brother and Sister did not say a thing.

Soon it was time to eat. Papa asked the children to run and get a big bowl to pour the soup in. They ran inside and brought back a bowl. Papa poured the soup into the bowl. The rock rolled out of the pot and broke the bowl! Brother and Sister did not say a thing. Papa looked at the rock. "That's not a turtle," he said, "What happened?"

Brother and Sister told their father how the turtle had tricked them into letting it escape. "It really played beautiful music," said the sister.

"And it really danced wonderfully!" added the brother. "But now we don't have any supper except for the bread," commented Papa.

"We're really sorry, Papa!" exclaimed both children.

The family shared the bread, and soon it was time to sleep. Brother and Sister crawled into their beds. Papa tucked them in. "We're really sorry, Papa," they said again. He began to leave the room. "Oh, Papa, will you open the window? It's a little warm in here."

Papa came back in the room and opened the window. Flute music spilled through the window from the forest and filled the room, beautiful music! "Papa, it's the turtle's music! It's the turtle's music!"

Their father smiled as he listened to the beautiful music coming from the dark forest. "If that turtle brings us music every night, maybe it's lucky you let it go. After all, nights full of music will fill us up more than a few bowls of turtle soup!" he said. And the turtle did keep playing its flute! They never saw it again, but each night when they opened their window, they could hear the turtle's beautiful song.

The End

Storytelling Tip (All Ages)

This tale has been written for the younger end of our target group. It includes descriptions of actions that make the acting out of the story more fun. If you are sharing the story with third or fourth graders, you may want to work from the skeleton and shorten the story. The tale is sometimes told ending the story with the father and his apologetic children sharing the loaf of bread without a mention of the turtle. Take your choice!

Activity: Acting out the Story (Pre-K–Grade 1)

This is a wonderful story to act out. As usual, name the characters and assign positions around the open space. Ask for additional characters. Sometimes children want to be the rocks or the cage or even the pot! You can also have a mother instead of or in addition to the father in the story. Of course, there can be many turtles and children as long as all the characters are represented.

Remind everyone of the three rules for acting out stories:

1. Listen to the storyteller!

2. Be safe!

3. Have fun!

Activity: Exploring Names in a Story (Grades 2–4)

None of the characters have names in this version of the story. They are identified by their position in the family. This provides an opportunity to explore how names function in a story. Ask the children these questions:

- Do you think having characters without names is a good way to tell the story? Why?

- Would it be a stronger story if the brother and sister had names?

  What should their names be?

- Would they have Hispanic names or Indian names? (This story most likely comes from after the European settling in the region.)

  Try it out. Choose names for the characters and retell the tale. Then ask:

- Do you think the story is better with the names?

- When the children had names, did you picture them differently from when you first heard the story without names?

- If we used different names, do you think it would change the meaning of the story?

- Would different names change the picture you have of the children in the story?

This discussion invites the children to explore the concept of names in a story rather than memorizing characters' names. It will help them understand how and why names are used.

 LITERACY CONNECTION: The discussion of names in a story builds **word awareness,** supports **writing skills,** and helps children notice how authors use names to further their ideas and themes.

The Skeleton for "The Tricky Turtle"

1. Turtle lives in the forest.

2. Turtle wakes up and goes to river to drink and play his flute.

3. A man in the forest is looking for food for his family.

4. The man hears the turtle playing the flute.

5. The man makes a cage and catches the turtle.

6. He brings the turtle home to make turtle soup.

7. He needs firewood.

8. He asks his son and daughter to watch the turtle while he gets firewood.

9. Do *not* let the turtle out of the cage!

10. Th father goes to the forest. The children watch the turtle.

11. The turtle says it can play flute if they open the cage.

12. They do.

13. The turtle says it can dance, too, if they let it out of cage.

14. They do.

15. The children dance with turtle.

16. The turtle sneaks into forest while children are dancing.

17. The turtle hides in a bush and stops playing.

18. The children stop dancing.

19. They look for turtle. No luck.

20. They put a big rock in a cage to try to trick their father.

21. The father comes back. He cooks the rock.

22. When the father pours out the soup, the rock breaks the bowl.

23. The children explain.

24. They only have bread for supper. Tricky turtle!

25. The turtle plays music from forest as the children go to bed.

26. The father thinks maybe music is better than a few bowls of turtle soup.

The End

From *Stories in Action: Interactive Tales and Learning Activities to Promote Early Literacy*
by Bill Gordh. Westport, CT: Libraries Unlimited. Copyright © 2006.

A hummingbird is a delightful little creature, and it's fun to learn how it got its beautiful colors.

How the Hummingbird Got Its Colors

When we think of a hummingbird, we picture a flittering little bird full of colors, hovering over a flower and then darting off in a flash. In those moments when it is still, the sun catches the reds and blues and greens and blacks and silvers—such a tiny bird with so much color! But the hummingbird used to be just plain gray, flying through the rainforest. Then he helped Puma. You may ask how a tiny bird could help a big cat like Puma. Well, this is the story.

Puma was walking through the forest one day when she stepped on Mouse's babies. She didn't mean to; they just happened to be in the grass where she walked. In fact, she didn't really notice. She just kept walking. But Mouse noticed! When she came back to her little ones, Mouse found them just lying there, crushed by Puma. She was mad! She went to find Puma. Mouse wanted to pay back Puma for the terrible thing she had done. Mouse found Puma sleeping. She had an idea for a terrible thing to do. She got sticky pitch from the trees and put it on the sleeping puma's closed eyes. She put dirt on the sticky pitch, then more pitch and then leaves. Puma would never open her eyes again! That would teach her to watch where she was going! Before she left, Mouse nipped Puma's ear to awaken her and whispered in her ear, "Next time, watch where you're walking! You stomped on my babies!" Mouse scurried off.

Puma woke up. She ope—no, she couldn't open her eyes! She rubbed her eyes with her paws. She still couldn't open her eyes. She roared! The roar filled the forest. Hummingbird was flittering around when he heard the roar of Puma. He was curious and flew until he saw Puma rubbing her eyes. "What's wrong?" asked Hummingbird.

"I can't open my eyes!" cried Puma.

"Please help me!"

"What happened?" asked Hummingbird.

Puma replied, "I must have stepped on Mouse's nest full of babies. She was angry and has covered my eyes with pitch and leaves. Will you help me?"

"I'll try," was Hummingbird's reply.

Hummingbird went to work. Up and down he flittered pulling away a stick, a leaf, some pitch—over and over and over until Puma could see again! Puma blinked and smiled. "What can I do for you, my little friend?" asked Puma.

Hummingbird smiled, "Oh nothing. Thanks."

Puma looked at Hummingbird flittering there with his gray feathers. Puma had an idea and suggested, "How would you like some colors?"

"Colors?" asked Hummingbird.

"Yes," said Puma, "Stay right there. Let me surprise you with some colors."

So Puma scurried off into the forest. She gathered green from the long liana vines. She found the blackest black from deep in a cave. Puma collected red from the urucu plant, grabbed blue from the sky and silver from the stardust. She ran back to Hummingbird and said, "Now you close your eyes." Hummingbird closed his eyes and Puma threw the colors into the air. They settled on Hummingbird here and there, all over his feathered body. Puma called out, "Now open your eyes. Look!" Hummingbird looked at himself. He couldn't believe it. He flitted and fluttered about looking at how the sun caught all his new colors! He was beautiful!

"Thank you!" cried Hummingbird.

"Thank you!!" replied Puma.

And that's how Hummingbird got his colors.

The End

Storytelling Tips (All Ages)

The story is presented with the fate of the mouse's babies unclear. Some very young listeners don't want to face the notion that the babies are killed, and for them you can use the story as presented. In some versions of the story, the babies are killed, and if you wish you can present the story this way. You should adjust the story according to your listeners.

Activity: Moving Like a Hummingbird (Pre-K and K)

You will need a box full of colorful scarves for this activity. After sharing the story, allow all the children to be gray hummingbirds flying around the room. As they fly, call out to them as Puma, "Thank you for helping me. I have something special for you."

Then take out a scarf and call one of the children by name. Hand her or him the scarf and tell where the color is from: "Here's some blue from the beautiful blue sky! Now fly with your color." Give out all the scarves, one at a time. You will wind up with a roomful of fluttering colors. An alternative or additional way to lead this activity is to let each child do a solo (or duet) hummingbird dance selecting several scarves of their choice and then returning the scarves after each dance.

 LITERACY CONNECTION: Providing movement experiences derived from a story allows the children to enact physically what they have been visualizing while listening. It reinforces **narrative understanding.** When they hear the tale again, they will bring the movement experience to the story.

Activity: Providing Colors for the Hummingbird (Grades 2–4)

Following the story, share some pictures of hummingbirds that show their colors clearly. Have the class name the colors they find. List the colors on the board or a chart. Where would Puma go to find these colors? From the class's understanding of the rainforest, have them suggest sources for the colors given to Hummingbird.

 LITERACY CONNECTION: The experience of working from photographs supports the growth of the student's descriptive powers and their ability to notice details of colors and size. They can then apply these to a story and build **narrative skills.**

This story is a "Why" story and can be used in tandem with the "Why" story exploration in Chapter 12.

The Skeleton for "How Hummingbird Got His Colors"

1. Puma walks through the forest.

2. Puma steps on a nest of mice babies.

3. Mama mouse returns and finds the babies.

4. Mouse is mad.

5. Mouse finds Puma asleep.

6. Mouse covers Puma's eyes with pitch and leaves and dirt.

7. Puma cannot open her eyes when she awakes.

8. Puma asks gray Hummingbird for help.

9. Hummingbird picks out all the things covering Puma's eyes.

10. Puma wishes to thank Hummingbird.

11. Puma gathers colors from the forest and sky and throws them onto Hummingbird.

12. That's how Hummingbird got his colors.

The End

From *Stories in Action: Interactive Tales and Learning Activities to Promote Early Literacy* by Bill Gordh. Westport, CT: Libraries Unlimited. Copyright © 2006.

The stories presented in this chapter provide just a peek at the Amazon culture, but it's a peek that encourages students to find out more. Here are some picture books that may further your studies.

Thematic Picture Book Suggestions

 LITERACY CONNECTION: Having a selection of picture books to augment the exploration of Amazonian culture enriches the children's introduction to this topic. The stories they have heard increase **print motivation** and makes children want to investigate further.

Brett, Jan. *The Umbrella.* Putnam Juvenile, 2004.

Cherry, Lynne. *The Great Kapok Tree: A Tale of the Amazon Rain Forest.* Sagebrush, 2001.

Flora. *Feathers Like a Rainbow: An Amazon Indian Tale.* HarperCollins, 1989.

Gibbons, Gail. *Nature's Green Umbrella.* Harper Trophy (reprint ed.), 1997.

McDermott, Gerald. *Jabuti the Tortoise: A Trickster Tale from the Amazon.* Harcourt Children's Books, 1995.

Chapter 10
Learning about Northeastern American Indians through Folktales

The stories in this chapter come from the woodland tribes of the northeastern United States. Storytelling has always been an important part of the Native American culture, and these few tales can only hint at the wealth of the cultures of these people. This is true of any small collection of stories representing a large group of people. Nevertheless, it is a good start. Because the main focus of this book is building literacy skills, the activities are aimed more at that goal than furthering the study of a culture. However, these tales and activities can be used alongside the study of the music, homes, work, and games of Native American cultures.

Finger Play Warm-Up

Following the warm-up, have the children make frogs with their hands and hop them around in the air in front of them. (The children should not stand up.) Announce that all the frogs settled down next to the pond. Now you can begin the story. Their frogs will be ready!

The Frog Pond

A Folktale from the Abenaki of North America

Once there was a frog pond out in the woods.
It was full of frogs—some on rocks, some on lily pads, and some in the water with their big eyes just above the surface.

The frogs led a very happy life. **Their chief was an old log** that lay at one end of the pond. It never bothered them and there was always plenty to eat.

Then one day **a large white bird flew down** and landed in the shallow water. It had long legs. It had white

feathers and **a long, graceful neck.** The frogs had never before seen anything so beautiful.

They looked at this beautiful new creature. Then they looked across the pond at their chief, the old log. The log was not beautiful at all.

The frogs decided that they should make the bird their chief. They chose one frog to carry their message. The frog hopped over to the bird. The large bird looked down at the little frog. "We would like you to be our chief!" called the frog. **The bird nodded her fine white head.**

The frogs were so excited that they started hopping to celebrate. Some hopped on their old chief, the log. Others hopped rock to rock and onto the pond's bank. Night settled in, and the frogs sang for their new chief.

The next morning, there was silence at that frog pond. Why was it silent? Because there were no more frogs. Why? **Because their new chief had eaten up every one of them.**

The End

Storytelling Tips (All Ages)

Some children are upset with the sudden loss of all the frogs, so you might want to add a fly to the story. Because flies are to frogs what frogs are to great white birds, adding flies and having the frogs eating them at the beginning brings the food chain into the story. After you have told about the frogs' happiness in the pond, add that they are also content because there are always flies to eat. Make a fly with one finger (as in "The Fly's Castle" in Chapter 1) and let your frog stick out its tongue and capture the fly. Then make a chomping sound. Repeat this with the children joining the action. Then, when the frogs become the bird's dinner, it's a little less drastic. Another possibility suggested by my editor, Barbara Ittner, is that the frogs can quickly hop away as the bird tries to capture and eat them. They escape but realize their foolishness. This version brings up the same thematic concerns but lacks the dramatic finale.

In addition to adding the flies to the story, you can create a more dynamic scene at the frog pond. When the frogs look at the bird (an egret, by the way) they say, "Oooooooooo!" as they admire the beauty of the bird. Then have the frogs look at the log and say, "Uhhhhhhhhh!" Repeat both the finger play of the bird with the accompanying "Oooooooooo!" and the arm as log and the accompanying "Uhhhhhhhhh!" until the children have joined you on the "oooo-ing" and "uhhhh-ing." This makes the frogs' thinking dramatically clear and is great fun for the girls and boys.

Activity: Discussing Sad Endings and the Meaning of the Story (All Ages)

During the finger play of the story, the children cheerfully used their hands to portray hopping frogs; the frogs' demise is often not the ending children want. There are a few ways of addressing this concern.

- Talk about the meaning of the story. Why did the frogs get eaten? What should they have done? Why did they choose the bird? Was that a good reason for choosing a new leader? Is the ending necessary to "teach the lesson," that is, the tale's moral? Talk about all these ideas and the ideas generated by the children.

- Move to a discussion of the qualities of a good leader.

- After discussing the meaning of the story, you can ask for suggestions for alternative endings. Children may suggest that the frogs hid under the lily pads or hopped away to another pond and warned the frogs there of the danger.

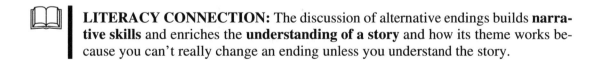 **LITERACY CONNECTION:** The discussion of alternative endings builds **narrative skills** and enriches the **understanding of a story** and how its theme works because you can't really change an ending unless you understand the story.

The following story tells of the origin of storytelling for the Iroquois and why they tell stories only in the winter months. There are many variations of this story. I chose this one because it gives the storytelling to everyone in the village. One of the goals of this book is to empower children to tell these stories. As you feel more comfortable sharing the tale, you can include other Iroquois stories within this story (see the activities following the story).

The Storytelling Stone

The snow was deep in the forest. In winter it was hard for the people. There was never enough food. The longhouse was quiet. The boy was far from the village. Everyone hoped the boy would be lucky in his hunt. That is why the boy was so deep in the forest. He knew that everyone was counting on him to bring back something to eat. Finally he caught two birds, both quail. He tied their feet together and carried them over his back. The snow was deep. It was slow travel.

After a while, the boy stopped. He was tired and cold, but there was still far to go. He saw a large stone. It was clear of snow. The wind had blown it clean. The boy climbed onto the stone and rested. The stone made a sound. The boy heard the sound but did not know where it was coming from. The stone spoke. It said it was the storytelling stone and that it told stories. The boy had never heard a story before and asked the stone what it meant by stories.

The stone was surprised, "You have never heard a story?! Stories tell you about the world. They tell you about the world you can see and the world you can feel and the world you can touch and the world you can imagine. They tell you about the beginnings of things. They tell you what and why and where." The boy felt warmer just hearing about stories. He said to the stone, "Well then, tell me a story."

The Stone replied, "I will tell you a story, but you must make a gift to me first." The boy shook his head and said, "But I have nothing. Well, I do have these two birds I caught, but they are food for my people." The boy grew silent. The stone was silent. The boy decided. He spoke again, "I will give you these birds. I would like to hear a story."

He lay the birds he had caught on the stone and waited and in a moment the boy heard a story, a story about a chipmunk and a bear having an argument about night and day. He forgot about the snow and his tiredness. He liked this story and as soon as it was over, he jumped from the rock, turned, and thanked the great stone storyteller and ran through the forest back to his village.

Everyone wondered where he had been. When he had not appeared for so long, they hoped that it was because he was carrying back lots of food, but they saw he wasn't carrying a thing. They looked at him, shaking their heads. "You have been gone all day, and you bring us nothing!" they said. The boy smiled. He spoke, "I did bring something, a different kind of food. Come into the longhouse. Gather around the fire and you shall hear." The people of the village followed the boy and they sat around the fire. He told the story he had heard from the stone. The words of the story filled their minds and warmed their hearts and when he was through, they wanted more. He smiled. He knew where he must go the next day.

And that is what he did, day after day through the long winter. Each day he brought something to the stone and the stone told him tales. Each evening the boy retold the tales to the people in the village. Day after day he listened. Night after night he shared the stories he had heard. Others found food for them to eat, and he brought the food of stories for their spirits. Then one day as the snow was melting and spring was near, the stone said to the boy, "Tomorrow I want you to invite all the people in the village to come. Tell them that each should bring a small gift. They will all listen to the Storytelling Stone!"

That night the boy told everyone what the stone had said. The people had never tried to follow the boy on his daily treks. They respected that it was his special place to listen and bring the stories back to them, but now that they were invited they were glad. The next day, everyone went to the stone—old ones, little ones, and all in between. Everyone brought something: a special feather, or doll, or rock. When they came to the place of the Storytelling Stone, they sat in a large circle around the great stone and each placed his or her gift before them. The stone spoke. It told tales they had heard the boy tell. It told tales they had never heard before. They heard about The Flying Head. They heard about the stars in the sky and the changing moon. Story after story after story. At the end of the day, the Stone was finished. "I am done," said the stone. "I will never speak again. Now you have the stories and you must be the storytellers. You will tell these stories to your children and your children's children. You will tell these tales and other stories, stories of events that happen to you, stories of your hopes and fears, of your dreams, stories of your ancestors. I have spoken." The stone was silent and it was a silence that felt like the whole world was silent and all the people rose and walked back to the village in silence.

The Storytelling Stone told tales in the winter, and so do the people of the Iroquois tribes. They tell all the stories but only in the winter, when the snow is deep and the spirit needs food—food for thought.

The End

Storytelling Activity: Becoming the Storytelling Stone (Grades 2–4)

After you have shared this and other stories in your exploration of Northeastern Indians, you can return to this tale and let students take turns being the storytelling stone. As the stone, they can tell tales including "The Frog Pond," "Why Chipmunk Has Stripes on Her Back" (the next tale in this chapter), and "Why Brown Bear Has a Short Tail" (see Chapter 12). Besides Iroquois tales, the children can tell other kinds of stories. Before they think about what story they will tell as the Stone, read to them again what the Storytelling Stone told the people: "You will tell these tales and other stories, stories of events that happen to you, stories of your hopes and fears, of your dreams, stories of your ancestors." This could make a wonderful setting for a dramatic presentation of why everyone should tell stories or for a cultural assembly.

 LITERACY CONNECTION: Providing a structure for the children as storytellers and a selection of stories they are excited about makes them eager narrators. Often the circumstance you provide is the key to the success of the children. When they are excited about a story, they develop more confident **narrative skills**.

The Skeleton for "The Storytelling Stone"

1. A boy in search of food walks in snowy winter woods.

2. The boy catches two quail.

3. He stops on the way back to village and rests on large stone.

4. The large stone speaks and offers to tell stories.

5. The boy has never heard stories before.

6. The boy gives the quails to the stone in exchange for a story.

7. The boy returns to village and tells stories in the longhouse.

8. People love the stories.

9. The boy goes back to the stone every day.

10. The boy tells tales to the people every night.

11. Winter is ending.

12. Stone tells the boy it is almost finished and that whole village should come following day.

13. Everyone brings a gift.

14. The stone tells stories to the whole village.

15. The stone encourages all the people to continue to tell stories.

16. The stone is silent.

17. People tell stories.

The End

As mentioned earlier, the following tale can be incorporated into "The Storytelling Stone." It's also a why story that can be reintroduced when you explore "Why" stories in Chapter 12.

Why Chipmunk Has Stripes on Her Back

One night there was an argument in the woods. It was between Bear and Chipmunk. All the forest animals were there, but the argument was mostly between Bear and Chipmunk. You see, Bear did not want to have daylight. He loved the dark of night. So he got all of his friends and they began chanting together:

Only Night!

Only Night!

Now Chipmunk felt it would be better to have night and day. So she gathered all of her friends and they began chanting what they wanted:

Night and Day!

Night and Day!

Over and over again they chanted their chants. Bear and friends:

Only Night!

Only Night!

And Chipmunk and friends:

Night and Day!

Night and Day!

But they did not take turns chanting their chants. They chanted at the same time!

Night and Day!

Only Night!

Night and Day!

Only Night!

On through the night they chanted:

Night and Day!

Only Night!

Night and Day!

Only Night!

Until …

The sun came up! Then everyone knew there would be night and day. Chipmunk and her friends were very pleased. She looked up at Bear. Bear was not pleased at all! In fact he was angry. Chipmunk took off! Down came Bear's giant paw and trapped Chipmunk. Chipmunk scrooched her way out from under the paw and then scurried up a tree to safety. But Bear's claws had made their marks on Chipmunk's back, and ever since that day, chipmunks have had special stripes on their backs. And we have had night and day.

The End

Story Activity: Chanting as Bears and Chipmunks (All Ages)

You can incorporate this activity into the story the first time you share it. Assign half the group to sit on one side of the space. They will be the Bear and his friends. Assign the other half to be Chipmunk and her friends. Pre-K and kindergarten children will want to tell you what animal they are as a friend animal. If you are keeping the activity geographically specific, you can discuss which animals live in the Northeast. Then the children accept it if they can't be a baby cheetah or a zebra and will cheerfully be a squirrel, deer, or possum. When it comes to the chanting part in the story, teach the chant to each group. By chanting, they will help tell the tale. When the sun rises in the story, if the children continue to chant, say, "And when the animals saw the sun, they all stopped chanting." This way, the story dictates the behavior and everyone will stay with the tale. Then add, "Now listen to what happens next. We aren't acting out this part." This will prevent the children-as-bears from attacking the children-as-chipmunks on the other side of the room.

 LITERACY CONNECTION: By having the children play parts in the story during the telling, they build **narrative skills** and become the storytellers. Their attention is assured, and by becoming part of the story, they experience and internalize its structure. The chanting the children do as the animals in the story increases **phonological awareness.**

The Skeleton for "Why Chipmunk Has Stripes on Her Back"

1. Bear and Chipmunk are having an argument at night in the forest.

2. Bear wants there to be only night.

3. Chipmunk wants night and day.

4. Bear gets his friends.

5. Chipmunk gets her friends.

6. Bear and friends chant, "Only Night! Only Night!"

7. Chipmunk and friends chant, "Night and Day!"

8. They chant all night until the sun comes up.

9. Then they know there will be day and night.

10. Chipmunk is happy.

11. Bear is mad.

12. Chipmunk runs.

13. Bear slaps down his paw and captures Chipmunk.

14. Chipmunk squeezes out and runs up a tree to safety.

15. But when squeezing through, Bear's claws scratch Chipmunk.

16. Now Chipmunk has stripes on her back.

17. And there's night and day.

The End

These are just a few of the many, many tales that come from the Northeastern United States Native American population. Of course, this does not include all the hundreds of tribes throughout America, but it is a good place to begin. Following are a few picture books that you may want to share, including the Algonquin "Cinderella." The Algonquin preceded the Iroquois as inhabitants of the Northeast.

Thematic Picture Book Suggestions

 LITERACY CONNECTION: Print motivation: after hearing the stories in this chapter and participating in the activities, the children will want to further their investigation of Native Americans. The following books can help do just that.

Bierhorst, John. *The Woman Who Fell from the Sky: The Iroquois Story of Creation.* HarperCollins, 1993.

Bruchac, Joseph, James Bruchac, and Jose Aruego (illustrator). *Turtle's Race with Beaver: A Traditional Seneca Story.* Dial Books, 2003.

Bruchac, Joseph, and Christine Nyburg Shrader (illustrator). *Gluskabe and the Four Wishes.* Cobblehill Books, 1995.

Martin, Rafe, and David Shannon (illustrator). *The Rough-Face Girl.* Putnam Juvenile, 1998.

Part Four

Exploring Structures of Stories

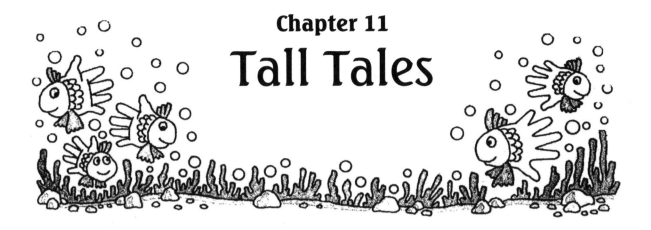

Chapter 11
Tall Tales

American folklore is filled with tall tales, that wonderful blending of true-sounding and exaggerated elements. Sharing stories of humorous, fantastical animals such as Paul Bunyan's big blue ox, Babe, is a fun way to begin an exploration of tall tales. Hearing about a specific tall tale animal inspires the children to create their own tall tale animals without addressing story structure. From this introduction, further exploration of tall tales can follow.

The animal tall tales told here are all fish tales, paving the way for the children to make up their own tall tale fish. The finger play that opens this chapter, "The Hand Fish" finds its origin in the waters of Lake Winnipesauke in New Hampshire. My daughter, Rachel, used to like to drag a little net in the water when we went canoeing. She wondered if she might catch something. She did: a hand fish! It's strange but it looked a lot like my hand! The following finger play tells a lot more about this amazing fish.

Finger Play Warm-Up

Begin with the finger warm-up. During the story when you first demonstrate the hand fish swimming thumbs up in the morning, pause for the children to try it themselves. Once you've done that, they will automatically follow the rest of the story with their hands as you use yours.

The Hand Fish

A Folktale from the United States

You may have never heard of Hand Fish but there used to be lots of them swimming the rivers and streams of America.

They were amazing animals and were called Hand Fish because they looked exactly like hands. They had some unusual habits.

One was that they always **swam thumbs up** in the morning
And **thumbs down** in the afternoon.

In the evening they would **swim palms up**
and when they slept they would still swim, but always
palms down. That was the best time to catch them.

People always said that if you saw a Hand Fish palm down
you knew it was asleep, and if you could slip a black glove on
it just before it woke up, you had it.

The folks that did catch them were usually quick and were
often jokers, so sometimes at a party you might wind up
shaking hands with a Hand Fish instead of a real hand!

Another thing that was quite remarkable about Hand Fish
Was how they worked in pairs. If a hand fish got hungry,
it would go and **grab some fish,** like a baby trout, and
**throw it to its partner. The partner would catch it and
throw it back into the first Hand Fish's mouth**—kind of
like baseball.

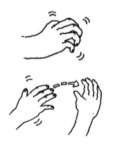

They loved watching one another do this, so you would often
see and hear pairs of **Hand Fish clapping for one another.**

Now with all these skills you would think that Hand Fish
would still be around. But there are still people talking about
that sad day way back when, when they waved good-bye to
the last of the Hand Fish.

The good-bye story goes like this:

Everything was going great for the Hand Fish until the Feet Fish showed up. Now the Feet Fish and the Hand Fish were not enemies, as you might think, but their habits did not work well together.

You see, the Feet Fish traveled on the bottom of the rivers and **their stomping** stirred up so much mud and dirt that **the Hand Fish couldn't keep a grip on anything.** When they lost that grip, they couldn't hold on to any food, and it was time to move on.

So the Hand Fish took off. Just picture it. People lined up along the river banks waving good-bye, and those **Hand Fish jumping out of the water waving good-bye right back.** It was a sad day.

Where they went no one was quite sure, though there is at least one report of a sighting out at sea. It seems a school of Hand Fish was swimming by a ship, when the order rang out, "All hands on deck!" The next thing they knew, the ship's crew had a deck full of Hand Fish!

I'm not sure that last story is really true, but it seems now you hardly ever hear of anyone seeing any Hand Fish. I sure hope they're okay.

The End

Introducing the Concept of Tall Tales to Children (All Ages)

After years of creating tall tale fish with young (four to nine years old) children, I have found that often they understand the concept of a tall tale before they can articulate it. After hearing these tales, many children who can't explain what makes a tall tale animal will tell you all about their own "Refrigerator Fish" or "Homework Fish." Once they have created a tall tale creature, they will "dive" into exploring what makes their own creations wonderful tall tales. Therefore, I begin by providing the experience of listening and creating.

That being said, you may prefer to lead with discussion, and the children you work with may thrive on the structure you have provided. If this is your preference, the notes following each of the tall tales suggest ways to guide a discussion of tall tales.

 LITERACY CONNECTION: The vocabulary related to stories and descriptions of story structure is important for children to understand because the **vocabulary** applies to many stories and understanding **story structure** contributes to **narrative skills.** Children may use the term for the type of tale, such as "tall tale," almost immediately after they learn it, but true understanding of what a tall tale is requires a number of stories and discussions.

Storytelling Tips (All Ages)

With younger children (Pre-K, K), describe only a few of the things the Hand Fish can do (the capture of the Hand Fish in a black glove is lost on some four year olds). Toward the end of the tale, when everyone is saying good-bye to the Hand Fish, describe how a kid stood close to the shore and gave the hand fish a high-five! Then do a high-five with any of the children who put up a hand (Most do!). It makes them feel more a part of the story.

After telling "The Hand Fish," move to a more "personal" tale, that is, tell a story as though it happened to you or someone you know. The personal tale is commonly used in tall tales to make the stories more plausible. When creating Tall Tales, mixing "fact" and "fiction" is the most challenging aspect.

Here's a story about my Uncle Knute (yes, I did have a great Uncle Knute) and his boyhood pet.

The Walking Catfish

My Uncle Knute was allergic to furry animals, but he really wanted a pet. So his mom brought home a baby kitty figuring maybe a young one wouldn't bother him. But when Uncle Knute pet that kitty, he sneezed so hard, it knocked all the windows out of the house. So she brought home a puppy for him. Well when he pet the puppy, Uncle Knute sneezed so hard, he blew the door off the hinges, and it slid down the hill. So his mom suggested a fish for a pet.

But Uncle Knute wanted a pet he could pet. "After all," said Uncle Knute, "that's why they are called pets, because you can pet them!" But Uncle Knute was a good thinker. So he got thinking about that fish idea, and he got a great "Knute Idea!" He decided to catch a catfish. "After all," reasoned Knute, "It swims near the bottom and has the name 'cat.' " So he figured he could probably teach it to walk! If it could walk, it could play with him. So he got his fishing pole and went down to the fishing hole and started fishing.

The first catfish he pulled up was a great big one. He decided it was too big and too old and that he could never teach it anything. He tried some more. The next one he pulled up was a little catfish—just right! He took it home in a little bucket and started to train it. He poked a little hole in the bottom of the bucket, so that the water would slowly drain out and the fish would get used to living outside water. So night after night, little by little the water went down, down, down until there was no water left in the bucket at all! And the catfish was OK!! In fact, it walked across the floor using its little fin-flippers. He named it Walker!

After that, Walker the Catfish followed Uncle Knute everywhere he went—to school, to the park, back home. Everything was great until one day a terrible thing happened. Knute and Walker were walking across a bridge, when the catfish slipped through a hole and fell down, down, down into the river and drowned!

The End

Exploring What Makes This Story a Tall Tale (All Ages)

It is really amazing watching children listen to these tales because they believe and don't believe the stories at the same time. When they hear the part about the catfish drowning, they want to find an explanation, because by the end of the tale they really like Walker. Depending on age, they will offer different questions and answers. Often a child will suggest that Walker forgot how to swim. Others will say that it can't be true. When you hear someone questioning the truth of the tale, you can explore the story backward to discover what makes it a tall tale. Don't announce ahead that you will try to define the tall tale, but rather explore the ideas with the children. When you finish, then you might talk about the nature of a tall tale. Here's how it might go:

Bill: Well, maybe it's not true that the fish drowned because fish don't really drown. But you believe the part where Walker followed Knute to school, right?

Children: No!

Bill: Well maybe you're right. Maybe that part isn't true. But you believe it could walk, don't you?

Children: No! And a fish cannot live without water!

Bill: OK, OK, maybe that part isn't true either, but Knute could be allergic to furry animals, right?

Children: Yes [and usually at this point, one or more children will tell about a relative who is allergic to furry animals].

Bill: And you believe his sneeze could blow out the windows, don't you?

Children: No, and not the door either!

Bill: Well, I guess it's just a tall tale.

Now you can have a discussion of the elements of a tall tale—the mixture of possibly true elements with fanciful ones. Create a Tall Tale Elements Chart. After the next story you can go back with the children and see if your chart also describes the elements of this new story. You might add elements to (or subtract them from) your list.

 LITERACY CONNECTION: Discovering and discussing the elements that make up a story help children build **narrative skills** and **comprehend** what makes the story work and what makes it a certain type of tale.

Following is the skeleton providing the key elements for retelling this tale.

The Skeleton for "The Walking Catfish"

1. Uncle Knute (or use another name) wants a pet.

2. He is allergic to furry animals.

3. He tries baby furry animals, but they make him sneeze [you can expand here if you choose].

4. He decides on a catfish.

5. He's going to teach it to walk.

6. He catches a catfish and places in a bucket.

7. He slowly gets rid of the water.

8. The catfish is all right!

9. The catfish learns to walk.

10. It follows Knute places.

11. The catfish falls in the river.

12. The catfish drowns.

The End

From *Stories in Action: Interactive Tales and Learning Activities to Promote Early Literacy* by Bill Gordh. Westport, CT: Libraries Unlimited. Copyright © 2006.

Instead of making the Tall Tale Elements Chart following the dialogue with the children about "The Walking Catfish," you might want to launch right into the tale of "The Light Bulb Fish." Then create your elements chart and go back over all the stories to see if the chart describes them all. To introduce the light bulb fish story say, "OK. Well, the Hand Fish story and the Walking Catfish story were tall tales, but listen to this next story. I know you'll believe it's true!" This story makes more sense to elementary age children than to early childhood age groups, but it is still fun for all ages.

The Light Bulb Fish

When I was in second grade, I really loved to read. I read all the time, and my mom was proud of me. But she did not like me reading late at night because then I was very hard to wake up for school the next morning. She took away my bedside reading lamp! Then one day a friend gave me a light bulb fish. She showed me how it worked. You see the light bulb fish lit up if you clapped three times. To turn it off you just clapped twice.

I took the light bulb fish home and showed it to my mom but I did *not* tell her what it could do. I set the fishbowl right next to my bed. I told my mom I wanted to look at my fish before I went to sleep. My mom kissed me goodnight. I had my book under my pillow and as soon as I heard her walking down the hall, I clapped three times! The light bulb fish turned on, and its light filled the room. I pulled out my book and started reading, but my mom heard the claps and came back down the hall to investigate.

I clapped twice; the light bulb fish turned off and I slipped my book back under the pillow. Then I pretended to be asleep. She looked in and then left again. As soon as I heard her down the hall, I clapped three times and the light bulb fish turned back on. I pulled out my book, but then I heard my mom again. Two claps! Lights off! Book away! This happened over and over again until my mother came in and said, "I keep hearing three claps," and clapped three times. Yep, the light bulb fish turned on and my mother knew what was up.

I pretended to be asleep and she did not say a word. She just picked up the fishbowl with my light bulb fish in it and walked out of my bedroom. She took it to her room. Just as I was really falling asleep, she called out, "How do you turn this fish off?"

The End

Storytelling Tips (All Ages)

When telling this story, place yourself (the "I") at the grade level of the children listening. If it is a mixed age group, use the oldest grade. Having the narrative in the first person is typical of tall tales and is more exciting for listeners.

 LITERACY CONNECTION: The first-person narrative suggests a model for children's tall tale story creations and the notion of author as narrator. Encourage children to create their own tall tales (see the activities that follow). This will build **narrative skills.**

The children enjoy joining the clapping to operate the light bulb fish. They are amused by the description of hiding the book under the pillow. You can repeat this sequence a number of times. It engages the children and builds prediction skills as they anticipate correctly what is going to happen. It also builds up the story to the point of the mother clapping her hands and turning on the light bulb fish.

If you are a woman telling the story, you might want to use a dad in the tale. It's nice to have a male-female balance in stories when you can.

The Skeleton for "The Light Bulb Fish"

1. A second-grade narrator likes to read at night.

2. His mother wants him to sleep.

3. Mother takes away reading light.

4. A friend gives him a light bulb fish.

5. The fish turns on with three claps and off with two.

6. Mother says goodnight.

7. Three claps—light bulb fish turns on.

8. The boy starts reading.

9. Mother turns around in the hall and returns to his room.

10. He stops reading and claps twice.

11. Repeat.

12. Mother claps three times. The fish turns on.

13. Mother takes the fish.

14. Mother can't turn off the fish.

The End

From *Stories in Action: Interactive Tales and Learning Activities to Promote Early Literacy* by Bill Gordh. Westport, CT: Libraries Unlimited. Copyright © 2006.

Activity: Creating Tall Tale Fish (All Ages)

After the children hear some or all of the preceding stories, they will want to create their own tall tale fish. Before they do, you can offer another step that will ensure the children are ready to join the activity. Use the room you are in as the inspiration for tall tale animal creations. At PS 203 in Queens, New York, the librarian, Jane Aaron, and I had great fun creating tall tale fish on the spot in the library and describing to the children what those fish could do.

Since everyone knows fish travel in schools, we told of a Marker Fish that wrote on a Blackboard Fish only to be cleaned by an Eraser Fish. Book Fish read themselves! Jane used to promise that the Cookie Fish would come the next session and hand out cookies. (The children always found cookies the next time, but the Cookie Fish had made its deliveries just before the boys and girls got to the library!) We talked about looking through Window Fish and walking through Door Fish. Soon the children were suggesting Computer Fish and Desk Fish and all kinds of other fantastical fish. When children are actively creating, it means you have given them a concept, a structure, inspiration, and the encouragement to explore their own ideas through this medium. By pursuing it as an oral activity, you and the children can ride on the energy and excitement that has been generated.

Activity: Creating A Tall Tale Fish Book (Grades 2–4)

Following the oral creation of tall tale fish by any and all children who wish to contribute, suggest creating a Tall Tale Fish Book. Having explored the ideas out loud, the notion of drawing and writing about these fish can be exciting rather than drudgery. After all, shouldn't creative writing be a joyful experience, an opportunity to share a great idea? Each child (or you can form teams) can name, draw, and write something about the tall tale fish on a piece of paper. Collect the sheets and make a book for others to enjoy! The second-grade children participating in my Early Stages program have come up with an amazing sea full of tall tale fish including the Dictionary Fish, the TV Fish, the Chair Fish, the Pointer Fish, the Underwear Fish, the Flying Rocket Fish, the Homework Checking Fish, the President Fish, the Game Fish, the Chocolate Teeth Fish, the Cupcake Fish, and, of course, the Storytelling Fish.

The nature of this activity allows children to participate actively in their creations at whatever level they are capable and comfortable working. The tall tale activity is not limiting. It is a springboard so children who wish to create a whole story about their fish are welcome to, and those who name a fish and tell something special about it in one sentence are successful as well. Both special needs classes and more "advanced" classes have created wonderful tall tale fish. The ideas and fun are available to all in tall tale fish creations.

 LITERACY CONNECTION: Children's creation of their own tall tale fish indicates their understanding of the concept and of the **narrative structure** of the tall tale.

Activity: Creating a Tall Tale Adventure with the Whole Group (Grades 3 and 4)

Creating tall tale fish can be great fun for the full range of children for whom this book was created. Older children can also make up tall tales about their tall tale fish. Creating a tall tale adventure is a bit more complex than inventing tall tale characters. It requires both an understanding of the way tall tales work and of the story arc. For this adventure, you can start with a familiar picture book that many of these children encountered as prereaders. Dr. Seuss's *And To Think That I Saw It On Mulberry Street* provides a wonderful step-by-step model for creating a tall tale story.

In his book, Dr Seuss describes in first person (like many tall tales) a walk down the street. Then page-by-page, he transforms one element at a time into something more fanciful. With older children, do not read the text but rather go forward picture-by-picture observing and commenting on the changes. There it is: the creation of a tall tale. In the middle of the book, the narrator comes to an intersection. On this two-page spread, there is only reality—none of the fanciful characters. It is a perfect time to point out how the best tall tales are always grounded in reality. By stopping at the corner of Bliss and Mulberry Streets, Dr. Seuss has brought us back for a moment, so that we will fully appreciate his tall tale adventure. Ironically the ending of the story has the narrator not even tell his tall tale once he gets home. He just reports to his father what he really saw.

Following the exploration of the Dr. Seuss book adventure, it is time for the group to create a Tall Tale. Call the story "How I Got to School." Begin the story at home with a tall tale breakfast. If no one is offering suggestions for the breakfast, ask a child what she or he had for breakfast. Because Tall Tales grow from reality, the children's own experiences will make the tall tales really work. If the child says, "I had a bowl of Cheerios," you might ask, "Since this is a tall tale, how big was the bowl?" or "Did you add any tall tale fruit?" You might ask if anyone else joined her for breakfast. These questions should be asked of the whole group. They are not to put anyone on the spot but rather to encourage everyone to have fun with their own imaginative powers. Often "the kid who always has something to say" will pipe up. In this circumstance, it is welcomed, for all you need is one idea from one of the children to get the story rolling.

The structure of the tale is simple:

1. You get up.

2. You travel to school.

3. You arrive at school.

That's the whole thing! But *how* do you travel? What do you see on the way? Who do you see, and what do they do? Just as the Dr. Seuss model illustrates, one begins with reality. If the children walked, then make the tale a walking tale. If they ride a school bus, something can happen in or to the school bus. Ask questions. The questions will add detail to the fun. Questions such as, "Which seat did you sit on in the bus?" "How far is it to school?" and "What did you bring with you?" will help the tall tale grow.

The tall tale will grow taller and taller as the children become more involved in the creative process. When the tale is completed, sometimes it is best to leave it as a great oral creation. Other times you will sense that it will grow more by turning it into a book-making project. This project can take any number of forms:

• The children can write down and illustrate the group's tall tale.

• Each child can make his or her own illustrated "Going to School" Tall Tale, and you can compile them into one volume.

• Each child's story can be created as a book.

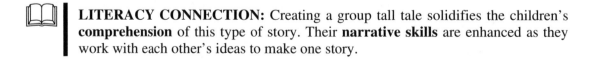

LITERACY CONNECTION: Creating a group tall tale solidifies the children's **comprehension** of this type of story. Their **narrative skills** are enhanced as they work with each other's ideas to make one story.

The Tall Tale fish exploration can move to other types of tall tale animals. The "Going to School" tall tale can set the stage for all kinds of other tall tale adventure creations, such as "My Camping Adventure," "Winter Vacation," or "Traveling across the Country." It can also set the stage for learning more about the legendary American tall tale characters like Paul Bunyan, Pecos Bill, and Annie Christmas.

And did I ever tell you about the "Sidewalk Fish"?

Thematic Picture Book Suggestions

 LITERACY CONNECTION: Besides introducing a number of great tall tales and setting the children up to create their own, this chapter used a Dr. Seuss book as a model for story creations. This builds **print awareness** and **print motivation.** The following books take them even further, and they will welcome the opportunity.

dePaola, Tomie. *Jamie O'Rourke and the Big Potato: An Irish Folktale.* Putnam, 1992.

Dr. Seuss. *And to Think That I Saw It on Mulberry Street.* Random House, 1937.

Isaacs, Anne, and Paul O. Zelinsky (illustrator). *Swamp Angel.* Dutton Books, 1994.

Kellogg, Steven, and Laura Robb. *Pecos Bill.* Harper Trophy, 1992.

Robinson, Fay, and Wayne Anderson. *Faucet Fish.* Dutton's Children, 2005.

Wood, Audrey, and David Shannon (illustrator). *The Bunyans.* Blue Sky Press, 1996.

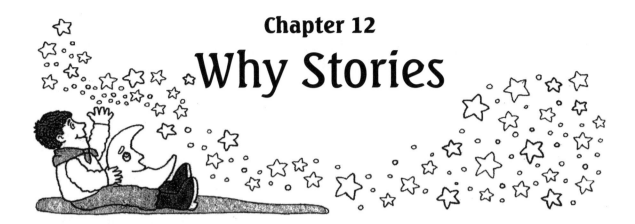

Chapter 12
Why Stories

"Why" stories come to us from almost every (and very likely *every*) culture in the world. People are curious animals. They wonder about the way things are. They notice things. They ask questions, "why questions." Sometimes the "real" scientific explanation does not reflect their experience or knowledge base. Their answers combine observation and belief. These stories sometimes are used not to suggest why something is the way it is but to "teach a lesson" or provide a model for behavior. Some "why" stories are told just for the fun of a good story. They often offer imaginative leaps that we would not consider in a million years, like our first "why" story from aboriginal Australia.

The exploration of the structure and creation of "why" stories is aimed at second, third, and fourth graders. However, these stories will delight younger children, and many of the activities, such as acting out the story, suggested in earlier chapters can be used with these stories as well. If you are working with younger children, go directly to the finger play.

From Making Observations to Asking "Why" Questions (Grades 2–4)

 LITERACY CONNECTION: Providing a discussion before the study of a tale type will help the children know how to **listen** to the story you share. This will lead them toward a more complete **comprehension** of the nature of this kind of story and will build **narrative skills.**

Before sharing the finger play about the moon, begin your exploration of "why" stories by asking some questions. It is important that the children realize "why" stories grow from observations. They will understand this idea better if they experience it as well as hear about it.

Bill: I'm going to tell a "why" story about the moon. When you look at the moon, what do you notice?

Children: The moon is bright!

Bill: That's a good observation. So we could have a story called "Why the Moon Is Bright." That might make a nice story, but it is not the story I'm going to share.

Children: The moon is white!

Bill: So that would make the title, "Why the Moon Is White." That's another good idea, but it is not the story I'm going to share.

[The discussion continues. Slowly, the children move their observations into "why" questions or suggest the idea as a title.]

Children: "Why the Moon is Round."

Bill: That would make a good story too, and it is close to the story I'm going to tell. Let me ask you this, Does the moon always look like it's round?

Children: No; sometimes the moon looks smaller! Sometimes it's a crescent! There's a half moon too! [A variety of observations will flow.]

Bill: And that is what my story is about. It's sometimes called "Why the Moon Changes Shape" or "Why the Moon Gets Smaller."

This dialogue can be longer or shorter according to the age and attention span of the group you're working with. The important thing is for the children to experience the genesis of these tales and realize that the "why" questions come from observations.

Finger Play Warm-Up

After the warm-up, say, "For this story, we use our whole hand as a moon. Now let it roll 'round and 'round. Now we can begin!"

Why the Moon Gets Smaller

A Folktale from Australia

Long, long ago, there was a land
where moons lived—**lots and lots of big,
round, rolling moons.**
The land was green and beautiful
and the moons just rolled around.

One night, **one of the moons got rolling
very fast. It rolled up a hill and into the
sky. Then it crossed the sky.**

On the other side of the sky lived a giant.
This giant had a great big knife made of flint.

When the moon had crossed the sky, **he took it** and carved off a little slice.

Then the giant took that slice, chopped it into tiny pieces and threw them into the sky. They became stars.

Each night the moon came back across the sky and each night the giant waited with his great big knife.

When the moon got close, the giant took it down and sliced off a bit.

Then he chopped up the slice and threw the new stars into the sky.

The moon got smaller

and smaller

and smaller

until there was no moon at all left in the sky.

Then another of those moons in the land of moons rolled up the side of the mountain and across the sky.

The big old giant was there waiting with his great big knife.

This still happens night after night, month a

And that is why there are so many stars in the sky,

And why during each month,

the moon gets smaller

and smaller

and smaller

until there is no moon at all left in the sky.

The End

Storytelling Tips (All Ages)

With this story, an alternative to strictly following the storyteller-told narrative as above is to let the children help tell the story by answering your questions. After you have taken the moon across the sky a couple of times, you can say,

> **Bill:** And the next night the moon is smaller. And it comes across the sky, across the sky and ... who's waiting?
>
> **Children:** "The Giant!"

[Who else could it be? The giant is the only character in the story, but the children do not think of it that way and enjoy knowing the answer and helping tell the story.]

> **Bill:** Right! The giant and he takes the moon down and … etc.

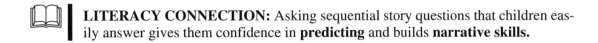 **LITERACY CONNECTION:** Asking sequential story questions that children easily answer gives them confidence in **predicting** and builds **narrative skills.**

Storytelling Tips (Pre-K and K)

You may find that some younger children are not comfortable with the giant and knife image, so for them introduce the giant alone. Then add the knife after you have told that the giant took the moon down out of the sky, "And when he brings the moon down, he takes out a big flint knife and cuts a sliver from the moon like someone might slice an apple." This tends to defuse any anxiety. With the youngest children, don't mention the word "knife" again; just describe the action of taking the moon and slicing it. Because the children are enacting the story with you, they enjoy the chopping and tossing of the stars. Allowing the children to join in on the action further allays any fears.

With the older children, hearing about a giant with a big flint knife adds a little excitement to the tale and makes them curious about what the giant is going to do. For them, use either way of telling the story or a combination.

Activity: Telling the Story with Only Gestures (All Ages)

This story is another of the finger plays in this book that can be told without words. The gestures tell the whole story! After your group has told the story a number of times, come back to it and suggest telling the tale with just gestures. They marvel at a story making sense without words, and if you haven't already done a gesture-only tale, they may suggest trying the technique with other stories.

 LITERACY CONNECTION: The discovery that gestures can tell a story furthers children's understanding of the **story structure** and of what is essential for the meaning of a tale. It also builds **narrative skills.**

From Making Observations, to Asking "Why" Questions, to Starting a Story (Grades 2–4)

Having begun with a story of the moon, it's fun to follow with another tale of the sky. By telling a story from a different culture, the children begin to see the commonality of being human and that asking questions about what we observe is a human trait. They also begin to see that every culture uses stories to communicate its ideas. Because this is a longer story, keep the prestory discussion shorter. Before the preceding story, you generated observations that could be the basis for "why" stories. For this tale, you can continue collecting observations and turn them into story titles and also consider how each story could begin.

> **Bill:** The next "why" story is also about the moon. In fact, it's about the sun and the moon. This story is from West Africa. Think about the sun and moon. What could be a "why" story about them?

Children: Why the sun and moon are in the sky!

Bill: That's right. That is exactly what the story is about! So let's think about how this story is going to start. If the sun and moon end up in the sky, where are they at the beginning of the story?

Children: In outer space?

Bill: That's a possibility and could make a great story, but that's not where this African story starts. Where else might the sun and moon begin?

Children: On the ground!

Bill: And that is exactly how this story begins.

 LITERACY CONNECTION: Using dialogue with children when exploring these stories makes them part of the **narrative process.** The work is more meaningful to them than when you present the material without including them.

Why Sun and Moon Are in the Sky

A Tale from West Africa

Long ago Sun and Moon lived down here on Earth. Their best friend was Water, and every day they went to Water's house to play.

And they played and played and played all day

Played and played all day.

At the end of the day, Sun sang to Water,

"Oh Water, oh Water,

Won't you come to my house tomorrow?"

But Water didn't say anything. Sun and Moon looked at each other, shrugged their shoulders, and began to walk home. Water quickly called out to them. "Oh Sun, Moon, you're my best friends. Won't you come to my house tomorrow?" Sun and Moon called back, "OK."
The next day, Sun and Moon went back to water's house.

And they played and played and played all day

Played and played all day.

At the end of the day, Moon sang to Water,

"Oh Water, oh Water,

Won't you come to my house tomorrow?"

But Water didn't say anything. Sun and Moon looked at each other, shrugged their shoulders, and began to walk home. Water quickly called out to them. "Oh Sun, Moon, you're my best friends. Won't you come to my house tomorrow?" Sun and Moon called back, "OK."
This went on day after day until finally one day Sun and Moon *both* sang,

"Oh Water, oh Water,

Won't you come to my house tomorrow?"

When Water didn't answer, Moon said, "If you are really such a great friend, you would at least answer our question."

Water replied, "Well, I didn't want to hurt your feelings and you see, your house is too small. So, will you come to my house tomorrow?" Sad Sister Moon looked at her brother and they both said, "OK."

Sun and Moon walked slowly home. Suddenly, Moon got an idea! "Brother Sun," she said, "you know what good builders we are. Let's build a bigger house!"

Sun smiled and shouted, "OK! Think we can do it tonight?"

"Sure!" replied Moon, and they ran home, got out their hammers, got out their saws, and got to work.

Hammer, Hammer, Hammer

Hammer, Hammer, Hammer

Hammer, Hammer, Hammer

Build a big house.

And they built a gigantic house! The next day, they went back to Water's house.

And they played and played and played all day.

Played and played all day.

At the end of the day, just for fun they sang to Water,

"Oh Water, oh Water,

Won't you come to my house tomorrow?"

Water said, "I told you, your house is too small!" Sun and Moon smiled, "Not anymore. We just built a gigantic house. Will you come?"

"I'd love to," said Water. "I'll be there at 10:00 o'clock. Can I bring my cousins and nephews and all?"

"Sure!" said Sun and Moon, "There's plenty of room!"

The next morning at 10:00 there was a KNOCK, KNOCK, KNOCK on the door. "Who is it?" called the smiling Sun and Moon.

"Water, can I come in?"

"Sure" said Sun and Moon, and they opened the door. SWOOOSH! A big wave of the ocean came sweeping into the big house quickly covering the floor and beginning to rise. "Yiii!" cried Sun and Moon as they climbed onto the table. There was another KNOCK, KNOCK, KNOCK on the door. "Who is it?" cried Sun and Moon. "More Water, can we come in?"

Sun and Moon looked at each other. What could they do? They had invited water to come with all its cousins. "Sure!" they called back and the door opened again.

SWOOSH! Another gigantic wave swept into the house. In the wave were dolphins and hammerheads and all kinds of other fish. Sun and Moon quickly climbed up onto a cabinet and watched their house fill with Water. KNOCK, KNOCK, KNOCK! "Who is it?" called Sun and Moon.

"More Water, can we come in?"

"Sure" cried Sun and Moon, and as more water and more fish swam through their house Sister Moon and Brother Sun climbed onto the roof.

KNOCK, KNOCK, KNOCK! "Who is it?" called Sun and Moon.

"More Water, can we come in?"

"Sure," cried Sun and Moon. As the water surged through their house and began to cover the roof, there was only one place for Sun and Moon to go—and that was up into the sky.

And that's exactly what they did. Sun and Moon climbed into the sky, and when they got there they looked down upon the water. Sun exclaimed, "No wonder Water said our house was too small. Water is huge. Too big for any house. Hey, Moon, it's beautiful up here. I think we should stay."

"Good idea," said Moon, "We can watch over our good friend from here!" Then Moon got a little worried, "but I think Water might get lonely at night."

Sun said, "You're right, Sister but what can we do?"

"I know!" answered Moon, "You can watch over Water during the day and I'll watch over Water at night!"

Sun smiled, "That's a great idea," he said.

And that's how it's been ever since. Sun watches down on his friend in the daytime and Moon at night. And once in a while when she really misses her brother, Moon comes over to the daytime sky to say hello. That's why, once in a while, you see the moon during the day.

The End

Storytelling Tips (All Ages)

In the traditional telling of this folktale, Sister Moon stays home and Brother Sun plays with Water. For young children hearing this story, it's nice to have all three characters actively participate in the whole story. This change does not affect the meaning or outcome of the tale.

There are a series of refrains in the story. They incorporate repeated words that can be sung or chanted in rhythm. These refrains give children something to latch on to when listening to a story. After all, they are not looking at pictures, and rhyme and rhythm help keep them engaged. Invite the children to join in on one of the refrains, and they will know they can join in on the others, just as they do with the finger play. The "play and play" refrain was created for preschool children. It can be shortened for early elementary age children.

 LITERACY CONNECTION: Participating vocally or physically in a story helps children feel ownership of a story and builds **narrative skills.** This boosts confidence in pre- and early readers' ability to **understand** the nature of story.

Activity: Acting out the Story (Pre-K–Grade 1)

This story is great for acting out, and the children can chant the refrains as they enact the story. You will see how easily these words stay with the children without them ever "memorizing" them. After following the usual setup, you may want to discuss how they will enact the water filling the house and the sun and moon's climb into the sky. They will dazzle you with their creative solutions.

• Ask the children to tell you the rules:

1. Listen to the Storyteller!

2. Be safe!

3. Have fun!

The Skeleton for "Why Sun and Moon Live in the Sky"

1. Brother Sun and Sister Moon live on the ground.
2. Their best friend is Water.
3. Sun and Moon play at Water's house every day.
4. Sun and/or Moon invite Water to come over the next day.
5. Water always refuses but invites them back.
6. Finally Moon asks why.
7. Water says their house is too small for Water.
8. Sun and Moon build a bigger house.
9. Sun and Moon invite Water to their big new house.
10. Water asks if it can bring its relatives.
11. "Yes!" reply Sun and Moon.
12. The next day, Water knocks on their door.
13. "Come in!"
14. The ocean comes roaring through the door.
15. The house starts filling with water.
16. All kinds of fish swim around.
17. Sun and Moon climb on table.
18. Knock, Knock!
19. Door opens.
20. More ocean.
21. Sun and Moon climb up on cupboards.
22. Knock, Knock!
23. Door opens.
24. More ocean.
25. Sun and Moon climb up on cupboards.
26. Knock, Knock!
27. Door opens.
28. More ocean.
29. Sun and Moon climb up on the roof.
30. Knock, Knock!
31. Door opens.
32. More ocean.
33. Sun and Moon climb into the sky.
34. Ever since that day, Sun and Moon live in sky.

The End

From *Stories in Action: Interactive Tales and Learning Activities to Promote Early Literacy*
by Bill Gordh. Westport, CT: Libraries Unlimited. Copyright © 2006.

From Making Observations to Describing the Ending of the Story

LITERACY CONNECTION: Leading a series of short discussions before the stories allows the children to **comprehend** one idea, hear a story as an example, and then be ready to further their **understanding of the narrative** line.

Following the two stories about the moon, you can move to animal "why" stories. Folktales with animal characters are a mainstay for children. They relate to the animals both as animals and as stand-ins for people. Acting out a story as a favorite animal makes the story come even more alive. Sharing these animal "why" stories will provide great models for the children's creations.

As with the previous "why" stories, you should begin with a discussion. So far we have gone from observation to question to how the story begins. In this discussion, you can add where the story must go. Here's a possible dialogue:

Bill: The next "why" story I'm going to share is about Brown Bear. What do you know about brown bears that could set up a "why" story?

Children: Why brown bear is brown!

Bill: That's a real possibility, but it is not the story I'm planning to tell. But if you were making up the story "Why Brown Bear Is Brown," how would it start? Once long ago Brown Bear was ...?

Children: White! [or purple or orange or black ...]

Bill: Great! And then your job is to tell something that happened to Brown Bear that made him brown. [You might welcome some story suggestions for this story.] What other "why" stories are possible for Brown Bear?

Children: [Will offer a number of possibilities, which you can appreciate and then discuss how the suggested story might begin.] Why Brown Bear Has a Short Tail!

Bill: That's it! And to start it off, what will Brown Bear's Tail be?

Children: A long, bushy tail!

Bill: Right!

[The children have discovered that you start a "why" story with the opposite of the trait you want the animal to end up with!]

Bill: Now here's the story. It is an American Indian story from the Iroquois tribe.

Why Brown Bear Has a Short Tail

A Tale from the Iroquois American Indians

Brown Bear used to have a long bushy tail and he loved it. He gazed at his tail with a smile, and he thought it was the most beautiful in the world. He thought, "My tail is more beautiful than any other animal's." He walked through the woods and he saw Chipmunk. Brown Bear shook his head and sighed, "You poor little chipmunk with that tiny little tail, and me with my big, brown bushy beautiful tail! Take a look, isn't my tail just wonderful?"

Chipmunk looked, squeaked angrily, and scampered up the tree. Brown Bear walked on. He stopped when he saw Deer. He noticed her tail, "Oh you poor dear Deer. You run so beautifully. But your tail must make you sad. But don't worry, you can still enjoy a big, brown, bushy beautiful tail by looking at mine!" Deer gave Brown Bear one look and ran off.

Every day Brown Bear wandered through the woods, comparing his big, brown bushy beautiful tail with everyone else's. The animals were tired of Bear's bragging, but Bear did not stop. It seemed no matter what was the subject, it would remind Brown Bear of his big, brown bushy beautiful tail.

Winter came and one day Brown Bear was walking through the deep snow when he saw Rabbit. She had two fish hanging from a line flung over her back. Brown Bear loved fresh fish and wondered how Rabbit caught fish in the middle of the winter. Brown Bear called out, "Hey, Rabbit, how did you catch those fish?" But before Rabbit could answer, Brown Bear added, "By the way, Rabbit, did you happen to notice how my big, brown bushy beautiful tail looks against the white snow? It must make you sad to have such a little cotton tail."

This made Rabbit angry, but it also gave her an idea. She answered, "Brown Bear, I caught these two fish with my little cottontail." (She had really used a stick and a fishing line, and thrown the stick in the woods when she was done.)

Brown Bear could not believe what he heard. "What?" he exclaimed.

"That's right," continued Rabbit, "It's a little trick I have." Now Brown Bear asked Rabbit in a very sweet voice, "Would you show me how to catch fish?" Then Brown Bear added, "Because, if you caught two fish with that little white cotton tail, just imagine what I will catch with my big brown beautiful bushy tail!"

Rabbit nodded, "You might catch every fish in the lake!! Come on. I'll show you."

Together they walked to the frozen lake. Rabbit lead Brown Bear across the ice to the middle of the lake. Then as Brown Bear watched, Rabbit dug a hole in the ice.

"Now what?" asked Brown Bear.

"Well," replied Rabbit, "The way I did it was that I squatted down and stuck my little tail through the ice hole. Then I moved my tail very slowly back and forth. When I felt a bite, I hopped up and pulled the fish out of the lake. It dropped off my tail and flipped around on the ice. I grabbed it. Then I did the same thing again."

"If that's what you did," said Brown Bear, "that's what I'll do, *but* I'm not going to jump up so quickly. I want to catch lots of fish!" So Brown Bear lowered his tail down through the ice into the cold lake water. "Ooo!" yelped Brown Bear. "That is cold!" He sat down on the ice with his tail in the cold water and began moving his tail slowly back and forth. He waited a while. Then he asked Rabbit, "Should I pull now?"

"Well," replied Rabbit, "You can but I think you would probably just catch one fish."

"No!" roared Brown Bear, "I want to catch lots of fish! I'll stay. Say Rabbit, will you tell me when to pull?"

"OK," said Rabbit "but I have to go home for a while. When I return I'll tell you to pull."

"OK," said Brown Bear, "Thanks!"

Rabbit hopped away. In fact, Rabbit hopped home, ate her fish dinner, and went to sleep! The next morning, she returned to the lake, and Brown Bear was still there sitting on the ice. Snow that fell during the night covered his shoulders. He looked up and asked Rabbit, "Is it time?"

"Yes!" called out Rabbit, "Pull!" Bear pulled and groaned, but nothing happened. He was still sitting on the ice. "Wow," said Brown Bear, "It must be a huge fish or many, many small ones. I can't pull them out. I better pull harder. You think so Rabbit?"

"I don't know. What do you think?"

"Definitely, yes," declared Brown Bear and he pulled even harder. He came flying up with a painful yelp. He landed on two feet and looked behind him to see how many fish he had caught. He did not see any fish, and he did not see his big brown beautiful bushy tail either. Brown Bear had pulled off his own tail. It was frozen in the lake. Brown Bear cried, "Oh, no. I lost my beautiful tail. I only have a little stub left. I have to hide." Off he ran until he found a cave. There he slept the rest of the winter, dreaming that he would wake up with a new tail just like his old big brown bushy beautiful tail.

But when spring came and Brown Bear woke up, he saw that his tail had not grown at all. He now had a short stumpy tail, and he's had one ever since. He went out looking for food. Spring and summer and fall passed, and when winter came again, Brown Bear with his short stumpy tail got an idea. "Maybe this time, if I sleep all winter my tail will grow big and brown and bushy and beautiful again."

So Brown Bear sleeps every winter hoping for a new tail in the spring. But does it work? I don't think so, and that's the story of why bear has a short tail *and* why bears hibernate every winter.

The End

 LITERACY CONNECTION: Phonological awareness. The repetition of the bear's bragging about his tail and the use of alliteration brings attention to the sounds of these words.

The Skeleton for "Why Brown Bear Has a Short Tail"

1. Brown Bear has a long, bushy tail.

2. Brown Bear always brags about his beautiful tail.

3. In winter Brown Bear sees Rabbit hopping by with some fish.

4. Brown Bear asks about the fish: Where did they come from?

5. Brown Bear makes fun of Rabbit's tail.

6. Rabbit decides to play a trick on Bear.

7. Rabbit says she caught fish in the ice with her tail.

8. Brown Bear wants to try.

9. Brown Bear thinks he will catch lots of fish with such a big tail.

10. They make a hole in the ice.

11. Brown Bear puts his tail through the hole.

12. He waits and waits until morning.

13. Brown Bear pulls so hard, his tail gets pulled off—it is frozen in the ice.

14. Brown Bear has a short tail.

15. Brown Bear is embarrassed and goes to hide and sleep in a cave until spring.

16. Double why—short tail *and* hibernation.

The End

From *Stories in Action: Interactive Tales and Learning Activities to Promote Early Literacy* by Bill Gordh. Westport, CT: Libraries Unlimited. Copyright © 2006.

From Observation to Story (Grade 2–4)

We're returning to Africa for the last story in this chapter, a "why" story from Kenya, East Africa. This is a special story for me because it was told to me while in Kenya by Kyalo Muasya, an Akamba. African animals generally stir up children's imagination. So this is a good story to set the stage for their creations. The story is about Ostrich. The ostrich is such a unique bird; you could have your group create a whole book of "why" stories about it! The conversation with the children follows the same type of exchange as described before. Now you can include all the parts of the "Why" story-making process:

1. Observation about the animal

2. Transformation of observation into a "why" story title

3. The beginning of the story: starting with the opposite trait

4. What happens to change the trait

5. The animal as we know it today

Bill: The next "why" story is one from East Africa about an Ostrich. What do you think it's going to be? What do you know about ostriches?

Children: [You will receive a multitude of responses because now the children understand the basis of this type of tale. Among the responses you'll get may be these:] "Why Ostrich Can't Fly."

Bill: That's a good one. It's not my story, but if it were your story, how would you begin? Once long ago …

Children: Ostriches could fly!

Bill: Right, and your job will be to tell what happened to Ostrich so that it could no longer fly.

Children: Maybe your story is "Why Ostrich Is Such a Fast Runner."

Bill: That would make a great story, too. It's not my story, but if you told it, how would it start? Long ago …

Children: Ostriches were very slow.

Bill: Excellent! And then you can tell what happened to make Ostrich such a fast runner. [If energized, the children might generate a whole story orally on the spot! You can continue collecting ideas about ostriches. You might even write them up on a board or chart. Eventually the long neck will come up, and then you can share the story. If they guess the long neck idea right away, you can acknowledge that they are right, but that you want to collect other ideas before you tell the tale.]

 LITERACY CONNECTION: The children should now have a clear notion of the nature of "why" stories, should understand the **narrative structure,** and will enjoy and understand the individual stories more profoundly.

Why Ostrich Has a Long Neck

A Tale from East Africa

Long ago Ostrich had a short neck. Every day he went down to the river to get a drink of nice cool water. One morning he took a drink, and as he drank he heard some moaning and groaning. Ostrich straightened up to see Crocodile swimming toward him. Ostrich backed up as Crocodile swam closer. "I won't hurt you," cried Crocodile, "I have a toothache! I need your help."

Ostrich took another couple of steps back and watched Crocodile as she swam up to the riverbank and put her big jaws up on the bank. Big tears rolled down Crocodile's face as she said, "Ostrich, my tooth hurts so much. Would you please look inside my mouth to see what's wrong?" With that Crocodile opened her great mouth and those big sharp teeth glittered in the warm morning sun. Ostrich looked at that big open mouth full of sharp teeth and took two giant steps back.

He said, "Crocodile, I am not about to look in that big mouthful of teeth. You'll bite me."

Crocodile shook her head and said in a very sad voice, "I won't bite you. My tooth hurts. Please look in my mouth."

"Do you promise you won't bite me?" asked Ostrich. "I promise," promised Crocodile.

"Well," said Ostrich as he took a step closer and peered into Crocodile's mouth.

"Closer!" exclaimed Crocodile.

"You promise you won't bite me?"

"Promise," replied Crocodile.

Ostrich stepped closer and with such a short neck he really had to stick his head way into Crocodile's mouth to see anything. "It looks …" but Ostrich did not get to finish his sentence.

CHOMP went Crocodile, and the smiling Crocodile had the Ostrich's head in her mouth.

"Let me out of here!" cried Ostrich.

Crocodile shook her head, "ENM-EMN!"

"You promised," cried Ostrich.

"Too bad," muttered Crocodile with her teeth still clinched.

Ostrich started pulling. He tried to pull his head out of Crocodile's mouth. But Crocodile did not let go, so Ostrich began pulling Crocodile out of the river and as he pulled his neck grew longer and longer and longer. Finally Crocodile was all the way out of the water, but she would not let go of Ostrich's head. The African sun beat down on Crocodile's back and finally she got so hot, she let go of Ostrich so that she could slide back into the cool river.

As soon as Ostrich was free, he raised his head and looked around. "Wow!" exclaimed Ostrich. It seemed like he could see for miles. Then he realized why. His neck was stretched. He had a very long neck!

And ever since that day, ostriches have had long necks. Besides that, Ostriches now only drink from watering holes. They stay away from the river where the tricky crocodile lives.

The End

Storytelling Tips (All Ages)

This story is presented with Crocodile as a "she" and Ostrich as a "he." You don't have to tell the story this way, but often children will assume that Crocodile is a "he" and Ostrich a "she." With many picture books continuing to go with very predictable gender assignments for animal characters (a ferocious animal like a bear will be a male; a kitten will be a female), in your storytelling you have an opportunity to keep a healthy balance.

The Skeleton for "Why Ostrich Has a Long Neck"

1. Ostrich has a short neck.

2. Ostrich goes to the river to drink.

3. Crocodile swims up to Ostrich.

4. Crocodile claims it has a toothache.

5. Crocodile asks Ostrich to look in her mouth.

6. Ostrich is afraid.

7. Crocodile promises not to bite.

8. They go back and forth.

9. Ostrich steps closer.

10. Closer.

11. Closer.

12. Ostrich puts his head in Crocodile's mouth.

13. Snap!

14. Crocodile won't let go.

15. Ostrich starts pulling.

16. Ostrich's neck starts stretching.

17. Ostrich pulls Crocodile out of the river.

18. The sun is hot.

19. Crocodile needs the water.

20. Crocodile lets go and slides back into the river.

21. Ostrich raises its head and runs away.

22. Ostrich now has a long neck.

23. Ostrich does not go near the river again.

The End

Activity: Creating Why Stories (Grades 2–4)

The children have now heard a nice selection of "why" stories. (More "why" stories appear in other chapters in this book and are referenced at the end of the chapter.) The natural culmination of the series of dialogues you have led before each story is the creation of original animal "why" stories. Begin with a group story created orally. Then move to small group or individual story creations.

Whole Group Activity (Grades 2–4): Following the ostrich tale, invite the children to think about other animals and "why" stories that could be created.

Bill:	Now let's create our own "why" story. Let's start with an animal. Who's got an animal? [Select someone.]
Children:	A cheetah!
Bill:	OK, what would be a good "why" story about a cheetah?
Children:	Why Cheetah is the fastest runner!
Bill:	Great. So how will we start the story?
Children:	Long ago Cheetah was very slow.
Bill:	And what happened?

Follow the raised hands to create the story. Generally the children build on each other's ideas. Occasionally children get so excited with their ideas that they don't really hear what someone else has said and offer an addition that doesn't make sense sequentially. You can pause and remind the child of what the previous storyteller said. If you write the story on a board or large paper, the sequencing is more visible. However, if you keep it oral, the children are called on to be more attentive listeners. Either method can be effective depending on the group. You may want to try both ways over two meeting sessions, one method at each session. By trying different approaches, children develop new ways of working and discover what is most successful for each of them.

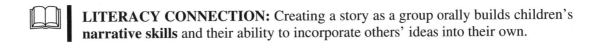 **LITERACY CONNECTION:** Creating a story as a group orally builds children's **narrative skills** and their ability to incorporate others' ideas into their own.

Small Group Activity (Grades 2–4): Following the whole-group story-making, divide the children into smaller groups. Your guidance of the whole group creating a story serves as a model for the smaller groups. The assignment for the small group is to make up an animal "why" story. You can move from group to group as a facilitator asking the right questions to move them along. When the stories are finished, the whole group gathers again for each small group to present its story. You can have each group present in the same way or let each choose their method of presentation. The presentations might include the following:

- One child tells the story from a story skeleton the group has created.

- One child tells the story from memory.

- One child reads the story that the group wrote down during the story creation.

- The group retells the story with a narrator(s) and actors portraying the characters.

- The small group reads an illustrated story.

You can offer the presentation choices before the groups begin their creative work or as you make your rounds. The advantage of waiting a bit is that the creation of the story remains the focus rather than including a discussion on how the story should be presented. Once they get their stories going, they can determine how they will document their story—as a skeleton, a play, or an illustrated story.

 LITERACY CONNECTION: Making decisions on presenting stories makes children aware of the needs of the presentation. This awareness helps them actively build their own **narrative skills.**

Individual Activity (Grades 2–4): After the whole group story creation, in addition to or instead of the small groups, you can move the story-making process to the individual. This project would most likely be in the form of a written and illustrated story. Depending on the age and abilities of the children, these stories might be half a page with one illustration or a little book with a number of pictures. The children can then read or tell these stories to the whole group. The individual stories can be compiled into a volume of "why" stories and made available to others.

 LITERACY CONNECTION: Creating a book makes the children authors and allows them to feel a part of the great world of books as a creative force. This builds **print awareness** and **print motivation.**

Creating "why" stories is a fun challenge for any age group. Try one yourself and you'll see. If you work with the same children several years in a row, you can continue doing "why" stories and change the themes. The animal stories are always fun, but you can also find "why" stories about the stars, trees, flowers, and fruits to share with the children as a launching pad. Over the years, you can accumulate volumes of all sorts of "why" stories created by excited, engaged, and imaginative children.

Other "Why" Stories in This Book

Besides the stories presented in this chapter, there are a number of other "why" stories in this book that you might want to use for this exploration:

- "Why Thumb Lives Apart" (Introduction)

- "Why Spider Has Crooked Legs" (Chapter 7)

- "Why Spider Is Bald" (Called "Spider's Stew Cap") (Chapter 7)

- "Why Everyone Knows Something" (Called "Spider and Knowledge") (Chapter 7)

- "Why Chipmunk Has Stripes on Her Back" (Chapter 10)

The fact that some of the other "why" stories in the book do not have "why" in their titles provides the opportunity to discuss why one might or might not use the word in the title. Then the children can use "why" in their own titles or not, depending on what they feel is best for the story. There are also many picture books of why stories that are useful to make available to the children during this exploration. The children will notice that many of them do *not* begin the way we have begun all of our "why" stories, that is, with the lack of the attribute as the opening of the story. This sets up a great circumstance for talking about the style of a story and how there are many ways to tell the same story. It also provides models for a variety of story openings.

Thematic Picture Book Suggestions

 LITERACY CONNECTION: After sharing the "why" stories and the activities in this chapter, the children will be **motivated** to look at and read books of "why" stories. The books provide additional models for the children's creations as well as allowing the children simply to enjoy more great stories.

Aardema, Verna. *Why Mosquitoes Buzz in People's Ears: A West African Tale.* Puffin Books, 1978.

Oughton, Jerrie, and Lisa Desimini (illustrator). *How the Stars Fell into the Sky: A Navajo Legend.* Houghton Mifflin, 1996.

Richards, Jean, Rudyard Kipling, and Norman Gorbaty (illustrator). *How the Elephant Got Its Trunk: A Retelling of the Rudyard Kipling Tale.* Henry Holt, 2003.

Salley, Coleen, and Janet Stevens (illustrator). *Why Epossumondas Has No Hair on His Tail.* Harcourt, 2004.

Chapter 13
Cumulative Tales

As with the "why" stories, cumulative tales are told all over the world. Typically these tales begin with one character trying to accomplish something. This character then meets a series of other characters one at a time. Each time a character is added, there is some story device that calls for the naming of all the characters that have appeared in the story so far. This continues until a final character through word or action either helps accomplish the task or does something to change the story. Although the study of the structure of cumulative tales and creating original cumulative stories is designed for second, third, and fourth graders, these stories are wonderful for younger children as well, and specific activities are designated for pre-K, kindergarten, and first grade children following the stories.

> **LITERACY CONNECTION:** As literacy builders, these tales incorporate **sequencing** as a **structural narrative** element and therefore support the growth and use of this skill for pre- and early readers.

Introducing Cumulative Tales (Grades 2–4)

The children should hear a number of cumulative tales before discussing their structures. Tell your listeners that you are going to share some cumulative tales. They will likely look at you with a puzzled look because "cumulative" is likely to be a new term. Assure them that they will discover its meaning through discussion after some stories are told. After sharing the stories, ask what they notice about the stories—what do they have in common? If you have not already used the finger play "The Fly's Castle" from Chapter 5, you might begin the cumulative story exploration with it. "The Fly's Castle" is a shorter and simpler cumulative tale than the following one and should be included in this study as well. "Sparrow and Crow" is a wonderful cumulative tale from India that will engage the whole group.

Finger Play Warm-Up

Following the warm-up and hands in lap, you can begin the story. The finger play is introduced in the first line with the crow, so the children will be ready to join you.

Sparrow and Crow

A Folktale from India

Once there was a crow in one tree
and a sparrow in another tree.
They both spotted something on the
ground and flew down.

Sparrow found a grain of rice and ate it.
Crow found a pearl, picked it up, and flew
back to his branch.

Sparrow wanted the pearl and called up to Crow,
"Crow, Crow, give me that pearl!"

Crow said, "No, why should I?"

Sparrow said, "Wa-a-a-ah! Wa-a-a-ah!
Crow won't give me the pearl;
And I'm left here crying!"

So Sparrow flew to the tree and said,
"Tree, Tree, shake your branches!"

Tree said, "No, why should I?"

Sparrow cried, "Wa-a-a-ah! Wa-a-a-ah!
Tree won't shake its branches;
Crow won't give me the pearl;
And I'm left here crying!"

So Sparrow flew to the woodcutter.
"Woodcutter, Woodcutter, chop down that tree!

Woodcutter said, **"No, why should I?"**

Sparrow cried, "Wa-a-a-ah! Wa-a-a-ah!
Woodcutter won't chop the tree;

Tree won't shake its branches;
Crow won't give me the pearl;
And I'm left here crying!"

So Sparrow flew to the Queen.
"Queen, Queen, lock up the Woodcutter!"

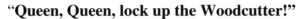

Queen said, **"No, why should I?"**

Sparrow cried, "Wa-a-a-ah! Wa-a-a-ah!
Queen won't lock up the Woodcutter;
Woodcutter won't chop the tree;
Tree won't shake its branches;
Crow won't give me the pearl;
And I'm left here crying!"

So Sparrow flew to Mouse and said,
"Mouse, Mouse, run up the Queen's leg!

Mouse said, **"No, why should I?"**

Sparrow cried, "Wa-a-a-ah! Wa-a-a-ah!
Mouse won't crawl up the Queen's leg;
Queen won't lock up the Woodcutter;
Woodcutter won't chop the tree;
Tree won't shake its branches;

Crow won't give me the pearl;
And I'm left here crying!"

So Sparrow flew to Cat and said,
"Cat, Cat, chase that mouse!"

Cat said, **"No, why should I?"**

Sparrow cried, "Wa-a-a-ah! Wa-a-a-ah!
Cat won't chase Mouse;
Mouse won't crawl up the Queen's leg;
Queen won't lock up the Woodcutter;
Woodcutter won't chop the tree;
Tree won't shake its branches;
Crow won't give me the pearl;
And I'm left here crying!"

So Sparrow flew to the dog and said,
"Dog, Dog, go bite that cat!"

Dog said, **"No, why should I?"**

Sparrow cried, "Wa-a-a-ah! Wa-a-a-ah!
Dog won't bite Cat;
Cat won't chase Mouse;

Mouse won't crawl up the Queen's leg;

Queen won't lock up the Woodcu

Woodcutter won't chop the tree;

Tree won't shake its branches;

Crow won't give me the pearl;

And I'm left here crying!"

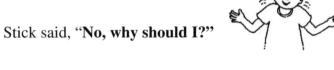

So Sparrow flew to Stick and said,

"Stick, Stick, shake at Dog!"

Stick said, **"No, why should I?"**

Sparrow cried, "Wa-a-a-ah! Wa-a-a-ah!

Stick won't shake at Dog;

Dog won't bite Cat;

Cat won't chase Mouse;

Mouse won't crawl up the Queen's leg;

Queen won't lock up the Woodcutter;

Woodcutter won't chop the tree;

Tree won't shake its branches;

Crow won't give me the pearl;

And I'm left here crying!"

So Sparrow flew to Fire and said,

"Fire, Fire, burn up Stick!"

Fire said, **"No, why should I?"**

Sparrow cried, "Wa-a-a-ah! Wa-a-a-ah!

Fire won't burn up Stick;

Stick won't shake at Dog;

Dog won't bite Cat;

Cat won't chase Mouse;

Mouse won't crawl up the Queen's leg;

Queen won't lock up the Woodcu

Woodcutter won't chop the tree;

Tree won't shake its branches;

Crow won't give me the pearl;

And I'm left here crying!"

So Sparrow flew to Water and said,

"Water, Water, put out Fire!"

Water said, **"No, why should I?"**

Sparrow cried, "Wa-a-a-ah! Wa-a-a-ah!

Water won't put out Fire;

Fire won't burn up Stick;

Stick won't shake at Dog;

Dog won't bite Cat;

Cat won't chase Mouse;

Mouse won't crawl up the Queen's leg;

Queen won't lock up the Woodcutter;

Woodcutter won't chop the tree;

Tree won't shake its branches;

Crow won't give me the pearl;

And I'm left here crying!"

So Sparrow flew to Elephant and said,

"Elephant, Elephant, drink up Water!"

Elephant said, **"No, why should I?"**

Sparrow cried, "Wa-a-a-ah! Wa-a-a-ah!
Elephant won't drink up Water;
Water won't put out Fire;
Fire won't burn up Stick;
Stick won't shake at Dog;
Dog won't bite Cat;
Cat won't chase Mouse;
Mouse won't crawl up the Queen's leg;
Queen won't lock up the Woodcutter;
Woodcutter won't chop the tree;
Tree won't shake its branches;
Crow won't give me the pearl;
And I'm left here crying!"

So Sparrow flew to Little Mosquito and said,
"Please, please, bite Elephant's ear!"

And Mosquito said, "OK,"
And started to bite Elephant's ear;
And Elephant started to drink up Water;
And Water started to put out Fire;
And Fire started to burn up Stick;
And Stick started to shake at Dog;
And Dog started to bite Cat;
And Cat started to chase Mouse;
And Mouse started to crawl up the Queen's leg;
And Queen started to lock up the Woodcutter;
And Woodcutter started to chop the tree;
And Tree dropped the pearl,

And Sparrow picked it up—
And smiled.

The End

LITERACY CONNECTION: The repeated listing of the characters and their actions as well as each character responding the same way builds **vocabulary** awareness and makes the children active and accurate **predictors** of the action. It makes the ending even more fun.

Storytelling Tips (All Ages)

This story offers a wonderful chance to use the sequence of gestures to further the excitement and understanding of how the cumulative story structure works. Sparrow flies to twelve characters for assistance. Depending on the number of children you have, one or more can be assigned to each character. Then use your hand-sparrow to fly to each character. Start it out like this:

Bill: In this story Sparrow is going to fly to twelve characters. I'd like you to be tree, you woodcutter…. My sparrow will ask each of you to do something, but you say, "No, why should I?!" Let's practice. Ready?

Children: No, why should I?

By naming the characters as they appear and describing what you need them to do, you have already revealed the sequence of the tale without making a big deal about it. They will be drawn in because of their roles in the story. As you go along, you can then teach the gesture for each character. So then every time you say, "Woodcutter won't chop the tree." The person playing the woodcutter shakes his head "no" while showing the chopping gesture. It's fun to enact the story with the children standing far apart in the room and have your hand-sparrow fly to each one.

The next cumulative tale follows a similar story path. Once again a bird wants something and goes character to character to try and get what it wants.

Magpie and Milk
A Tale from Turkey

Magpie loved to fly. With his beautiful black wings glistening in the sun, he loved to fly. Then he loved to relax and perch on a branch and look around. One morning after a nice flight, he was perched on a branch and looking around when he saw an old woman down below. She was milking the cow. When the pail was full, she went inside to get a pitcher for the milk. Magpie gazed at that pail of nice fresh milk. It looked delicious, so Magpie flew down and landed on the side of the pail to take a drink. The pail fell over and the milk spilt all over the ground.

Just then, the old woman came outside with her pitcher. She saw the spilt milk *and* she saw Magpie. Uh-Oh! Magpie started to fly, but the old woman was quick and grabbed his tail. The feathers pulled out, and she was holding Magpie's tail! Magpie looked at the old woman.

"Give me back my tail!" demanded Magpie.

"Well, fill up my pail with fresh milk," replied the Old Woman.

"Give me back my tail!" squawked Magpie.

"Fill up my pail!" demanded the old woman.

"Give me back my tail!"

"Fill up my pail!"

Magpie stopped. He asked the Old Woman, "If I fill up your pail with nice fresh milk, will you give me back my tail?"

"Yes!" declared the Old Woman.

So Magpie set off. He could not fly so he hopped. He hopped and hopped and hopped into the barn where he saw another cow. He hopped up to the cow and asked,

"Would you give me some milk?"

"What for?" asked the cow.

Magpie sang out,

Milk to fill the pail

So I get back my tail

And I can fly, fly, fly, fly away.

Cow said, "Sure, I'll give you some milk, but I need some tall grass to eat. Will you get me some grass?"

"I'll try," replied Magpie.

So Magpie hopped and hopped and hopped, hopped and hopped and hopped 'til he came to a field of tall, tall grass. He spoke to the field,

"Would you give me some tall grass?"

"What for?" asked the field.

Magpie sang out,

"Grass to feed the cow

So the cow will give me milk

Milk to fill the pail

So I get back my tail

And I can fly, fly, fly, fly away."

The field replied, "Sure, I'll give you some grass if you'll water me. Will you get some water?"

"I'll try," replied Magpie.

So Magpie hopped and hopped and hopped, hopped and hopped and hopped 'til he came to a water carrier. The water carrier had a barrel of water on his back and traveled field to field giving water to the field hands. Magpie spoke to the water carrier, "Would you give me some water?"

"What for?" asked the water carrier.

Magpie sang out,

"Water for the field

So the field will give me grass

Grass to feed the cow

So the cow will give me milk

Milk to fill the pail

So I get back my tail

And I can fly, fly, fly, fly away."

The water carrier thought about it and replied, "Sure, I'll give you some water. But I'm hungry and I'd love an egg for lunch. Will you get me an egg?"

"I'll try," replied Magpie.

So Magpie hopped and hopped and hopped, hopped and hopped and hopped 'til he came to a hen. He spoke to the hen, "Would you give me an egg?"

"What for?" asked the hen.

Magpie sang out,

"Egg for the water carrier

So the water carrier gives me water

Water for the field

So the field will give me grass

Grass to feed the cow

So the cow will give me milk

Milk to fill the pail

So I get back my tail

And I can fly, fly, fly, fly away."

The hen looked at Magpie and said, "You're a bird and I'm a bird so I'm going to lay you an egg." Hen started clucking and soon Magpie was hopping back to the water carrier carrying an egg. When the water carrier got his egg, he gave Magpie water and Magpie hopped over and watered the field. The field gave Magpie lots of tall grass and Magpie hopped to the barn and fed the grass to the cow. The cow gave magpie milk. It filled up the pail and Magpie hopped the pail full of fresh milk to the old woman.

When she saw the pail full of fresh milk, she smiled and gave Magpie back his feathers and helped him get his tail just right. Magpie looked at his tail, nodded to the old woman and sang out, "Now I can fly, fly, fly, fly away."

And that's exactly what he did.

The End

Storytelling Tips (All Ages)

You may want to show a picture of a magpie to the boys and girls. Sometimes children are not familiar with this bird, and it's nice for them to be able to picture the magpie on its quest.

 LITERACY CONNECTION: An illustration helps build new **vocabulary** and makes a word more meaningful and memorable.

After you say the little "Fly, fly, fly, fly away" refrain the second time, have the children repeat it with you. They will then be ready to join you when it comes around again and by teaching them the refrain, you have invited them to help you tell the story. You have also revealed to them that the refrain will repeat and they will anticipate their entry. They are also more likely to accompany you on the other repeated elements of the tale.

If you pause near the end of a line just before the word you'd like them to say with you, the momentary silence becomes an invitation. If they do not join you, just say the word alone, and they will probably join the next time you pause as you have demonstrated how it works. Like this:

"Water for the field, so the field will give me [PAUSE] *grass*

Grass to feed the cow, so the cow will give me [PAUSE] *milk*"

This pause used to invite vocal participation is a very handy device. I call it the "pausal invitation." You'll see it used again in the next story. This convention with pauses is one that the children pick up on, and once they do, they join in more readily.

LITERACY CONNECTION: Joining in on the telling of key parts of a story helps children internalize the **structure** of the tale and builds **narrative skills.**

Acting out the Story (Pre-K–Grade 1)

"Magpie and Milk" is a fun story to act out. Name the characters and point out positions around the space. Remind everyone of the three rules (Listen to the Storyteller! Be safe! Have fun!). Retell the story as they enact it.

LITERACY CONNECTION: Acting out stories helps children internalize the **structure** of a story and builds **narrative understanding.**

The Skeleton for "Magpie and Milk"

1. Magpie lands on a branch.

2. Magpie watches a woman milk her cow.

3. The woman enters her house to get a pitcher for the milk.

4. Thirsty Magpie sees the pail full of milk.

5. Magpie flies down.

6. Magpie lands on pail; pail tips; milk spills.

7. The woman comes out.

8. She grabs Magpie's tail.

9. If Magpie gets more milk, he'll get his tail back.

10. Magpie goes to Cow.

11. Cow wants grass first.

12. Magpie goes to Grass.

13. Grass wants to be watered.

14. Magpie goes to Water Carrier.

15. Water Carrier wants an egg for lunch.

16. Magpie goes to Hen.

17. Hen says, "Yes, I'll help you because we're both birds."

18. Magpie gives the egg to Water Carrier.

19. Magpie has water for the Field.

20. Magpie has grass for Cow.

21. Milk fills Pail.

22. Magpie has the pail of milk for the woman.

23. Magpie gets back his tail.

24. Magpie flies away.

The End

From *Stories in Action: Interactive Tales and Learning Activities to Promote Early Literacy* by Bill Gordh. Westport, CT: Libraries Unlimited. Copyright © 2006.

Continuing the Exploration of Cumulative Tales (Grades 2–4)

The word "cumulative" is both hard to say and difficult to remember. So use the word often during this exploration and ask the children to repeat the word. You can also solidify this new word for their vocabulary by playing forgetful, "Now, I'm going to share another of these stories, where the characters accumulate. What's that called again?" Pretending that you can't remember makes it more fun for the children to answer and help you.

 LITERACY CONNECTION: The frequent inclusion of new vocabulary in your discussions concretizes the word and its meaning for the children, building **vocabulary** awareness and skills.

The next kind of cumulative tale works a little differently from the preceding two. Instead of one character traveling to others, the new characters join the original character, one at a time, to try and complete a task. "The Fly's Castle" works this way as well. This offers another model for the boys and girls when creating their own cumulative tales. This is an old story from Russia and may be familiar to many of the children because it has appeared as a picture book a number of times. Here it is told a little differently in order to have the children participate in the telling.

The Big Turnip

A Cumulative Tale from Russia

Grandma and Grandpa looked out the window one morning. They could see the garden, and the garden looked great. The vegetables were ready to be picked! Grandma said, "We can make a nice stew from all those vegetables, Grandpa. You go on out and I'll wash up the pot while you get started picking vegetables." Grandpa smiled, grabbed his vegetable basket, and headed out the door, down the steps, and into the garden.

When he got into the garden he started by cutting some broccoli—SNIP-SNIP-SNIP and dropped them in the basket; SNIP-SNIP-SNIP and dropped them in the basket, SNIP-SNIP-SNIP and dropped them in the basket. Then he picked some tomatoes—PICK, PICK, PICK and dropped them in the basket; PICK, PICK, PICK and drop them in the basket. Then he snapped some green beans off the vines—SNAP, SNAP, SNAP and dropped them in the basket; SNAP, SNAP, SNAP and drop them in the basket. Then he came to the turnips. Now turnips are red and white and live underground with green stems and leaves sticking out above the ground. When you pick them, you grab the top, pull and POP!—out comes the turnip. So Grandpa started pulling out turnips. He grabbed the top and—POP!—out came the turnip, and he threw it in the basket. Then he grabbed another turnip top and POP! Out it came, and he threw it in the basket. Then another—grab the TOP and POP—out came the turnip and he threw it into the basket.

Then Grandpa came to a great big turnip, much bigger than any turnip he had ever seen. This was going to take some hard work! So Grandpa rolled up his sleeves, grabbed the top of the turnip, and pulled and pulled and pulled.

But [PAUSE] he could not pull that turnip out!

Grandma looked out the window. She watched Grandpa pulling and pulling. She opened the window and called to Grandpa, "Hey Grandpa, you need some help?"

Grandpa looked up and called back, **[PAUSE]** "Sure!"

So Grandma came outside and grabbed hold of Grandpa. Grandpa grabbed hold of the top of the turnip and together they pulled. They pulled and pulled and pulled.

But [PAUSE] they could not pull that turnip out!
A little girl walked by. She watched for a while. Then she asked, "Need some help?"
And they said, **[PAUSE]** "Sure!"
So the little girl pulled Grandma
And Grandma pulled Grandpa
And Grandpa pulled the turnip.
And together they pulled and pulled and pulled
But [PAUSE] they could not pull that turnip out!
A little boy walked by. He watched for a while. Then he asked, "Need some help?"
And they said, **[PAUSE]** "Sure!"
So the boy pulled the girl
And the girl pulled Grandma
And Grandma pulled Grandpa
And Grandpa pulled the turnip.
And together they pulled and pulled and pulled
But [PAUSE] they could not pull that turnip out!
A doggy walked by. He watched for a while. Then he asked, "Need some help?"
They said, **[PAUSE]** "Sure!"
So the doggy pulled the boy
And the boy pulled the girl
And the girl pulled Grandma
And Grandma pulled Grandpa
And Grandpa pulled the turnip.
And together they pulled and pulled and pulled
But [PAUSE] they could not pull that turnip out!
Kitty Cat walked by and watched for a while. Then she said, "Need some help?"
They said, **[PAUSE]** "Sure!"
So the kitty pulled the doggy
And the doggy pulled the boy
And the boy pulled the girl
 And the girl pulled Grandma
And Grandma pulled Grandpa
And Grandpa pulled the turnip.
And together they pulled and pulled and pulled
But (PAUSE) they could not pull that turnip out!
A little mouse walked by and watched for a while. Then she said, "Need some help?"
They said, **[PAUSE]** "Sure!"
So the mouse pulled the kitty
And the kitty pulled the doggy
And the doggy pulled the boy
And the boy pulled the girl
And the girl pulled Grandma
And Grandma pulled Grandpa
And Grandpa pulled the turnip.
And together they pulled and pulled and pulled
But (PAUSE) they could not pull that turnip out!
Ladybug crawled by and watched for a while. Then she said, "Need some help?"
They said, **[PAUSE]** "Sure!"
So the ladybug pulled the mouse
And the mouse pulled the kitty
And the kitty pulled the doggy

And the doggy pulled the boy
And the boy pulled the girl
And the girl pulled Grandma
And Grandma pulled Grandpa
And Grandpa pulled the turnip.
And together they pulled and pulled and pulled
But (PAUSE) they could not pull that turnip out!
Another ladybug crawled by and watched for a while. Then she said, "Need some help?"
They said, **[PAUSE]** "Sure!"
So the other ladybug pulled the other ladybug
And the other ladybug pulled the mouse
And the mouse pulled the kitty
And the kitty pulled the doggy
And the doggy pulled the boy
And the boy pulled the girl
And the girl pulled Grandma
And Grandma pulled Grandpa
And Grandpa pulled the turnip.
And together they pulled and pulled and pulled
But [PAUSE] they could not pull that turnip out!
Another ladybug crawled by and watched for a while. Then she said, "Need some help?"
And they said, **[PAUSE]** "Sure!"
So the other ladybug pulled the other ladybug
And the other ladybug pulled the other ladybug
And the other ladybug pulled the mouse
And the mouse pulled the kitty
And the kitty pulled the doggy
And the doggy pulled the boy
And the boy pulled the girl
And the girl pulled Grandma
And Grandma pulled Grandpa
And Grandpa pulled the turnip.
And together they pulled and pulled and pulled
And with all of them working together—
POP!!!!!
Out came the Turnip!

The End

Storytelling Tips (All Ages)

In this story, you will find the "pausal invitation" used for two different circumstances: following the offer to help and describing the results of all the pulling. They are printed in the text. The first appears like this:

"Need some help?"

They said, **[PAUSE]** "Sure!"

By including the pause the very first time, even before the children know what follows, the stage is set for them to join in the next time or the time after that. Soon they'll all join the "Sure!" following the pause.

The other pause follows the "But" that precedes the result of the pulling:

"And together they pulled and pulled and pulled
But [PAUSE] they could not pull that turnip out!
Because this is a long phrase, you may want to invite them verbally to join you the first time. So when Grandma has joined in on the pulling, after the **[PAUSE],** say, "Join me on this one." After that, you will only need to pause, and they will join you saying,
"They could not pull that turnip out!"

LITERACY CONNECTION: Offering children places within a story to participate vocally or with gestures helps them internalize the **structure, predict** upcoming results, build **narrative skills,** and enjoy the story more fully.

Activity: The Stew Making Game (Pre-K–Grade 1)

The Big Turnip provides the setting for some great activities that grow right from the telling. At the end of the story say,

Bill: Let's make turnip stew! Let's sit in a big circle. OK, now put the big pot in the middle. Now let's chop up the turnip, "Chop, chop, chop! Throw it in the pot."

Bill and Children: Chop, chop, chop! Throw it in the pot!

Chop, chop, chop! Throw it in the Pot!

Bill: OK. Now lets stir the stew. "Stirring the stew. Stirring the stew."

Bill and Children: "Stirring the stew. Stirring the stew."

Bill: Great! Well, we need more than one vegetable in the stew. I'm going to go around the circle and ask each one of you what you would like to add to the stew. Like this:

"Stirring the stew. Stirring the Stew

What would *you* [point with "spoon"] like to put in our stew?"

[The designated child then names a vegetable.]

Child: Carrots!

Bill: Do you want to chop them up or just throw them in?

Child: Chop!

Bill: OK. Ready? Chop, chop, chop! Throw them in the pot. Chop, chop, chop! Throw them in the pot. Now, Stirring the stew. Stirring the stew. What would *you* [to the next child] put in our stew?

Child: Broccoli!

Bill: Great! Do you want to chop the broccoli or just throw it in?

Child: Throw it in.

[By asking these questions, even the shyest child can participate by making simple choices, while bolder children can make their own suggestions.]

After adding all the ingredients, bring out a pretend stew cookbook to begin the set up for the next session's activity.

Setting Up the Transformation Game (Pre-K–Grade 1)

After the children have helped you make the stew, you can set up for another great activity that you will lead at the next session. It's called "The Transformation Game." Bring out your pretend stew cookbook.

Bill: Now let me get out my stew cookbook to choose exactly what kind of stew to make. [I pretend to open the book. I make a "ROAR!" as though it came out of the book. I shut the book.] No, we do not want to make monster stew! [Some kids will say, "Yes we do."] Let's see. "BOO!" [Close the book.] We do not want to make ghost stew! [You can do more of these if you wish. Open the book. Make a laughing sound.] Silly Stew!? Yes. Let's make Silly Stew. It says, "Add three shakes of Va-va powder." Va-va powder, what is that? OK, here's some Va-va powder.

Bill and children: Shake-a, Shake-a One. Shake-a, Shake-a Two. Shake-a, Shake-a Three.

Bill: Now what? "Add four leaves from the Lopteropta tree." Lopteropta tree? I never heard of that. OK. One leaf, two, three, four. Now what does it say?

"Let the stew cook for a week. Then let each child take a taste. He or she can then turn into any animal she wants to and move around the circle."

That is going to be something to see!

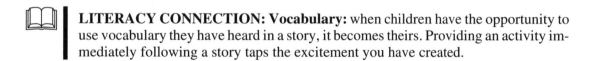

LITERACY CONNECTION: Vocabulary: when children have the opportunity to use vocabulary they have heard in a story, it becomes theirs. Providing an activity immediately following a story taps the excitement you have created.

When we first played the "Making the Stew" game, I noticed many children feeling uncertain about naming a vegetable to add. We often wound up with more turnips and a few carrots. At that time, the story (as in the picture books) never mentioned other vegetables, only the big turnip. So I added the picking of other vegetables to the beginning of the tale. In fact, when I tell it, I generally include a few more vegetables than are mentioned in this text. This provides the children with the vocabulary they need to actively participate in the stew-making game. The setup does not prevent a child who knows many vegetables from naming one that was not mentioned in the story. One of the goals of this work is to provide solid support for all the children listeners so that a shyer child can enthusiastically contribute. At the same time and equally important, it allows those who are creating more independently to take off with their ideas.

Here's another interesting observation of how this story is often presented: The grandpa comes to the giant turnip. He can't pull it out. Finally with the help of others, "POP!" it comes out. Although fun, the pay off does not quite work, because often the children do not know the sound of a regular turnip pulled out of the ground. So the "POP!" at the end has no meaningful context. By having the children help you collect vegetables with Grandpa at the beginning, the boys and girls make sounds and associate those sounds with what the vegetables do. That is why we pick some small turnips and make the "Pop!" sound. It gives the children all the information they need to really understand and enjoy the story.

The story and the stew-making activity are enough for one session. At the following session, re-tell "The Big Turnip" (See below) and then play The Transformation Game.

Retelling the Tale to Build Sequencing Skills (Pre-K–Grade 1)

When retelling the story of the big turnip, you will find the children ready to join you following the "pausal invitations" for "Sure!" and "They could not pull that turnip out!" You can use this participation to invite them further into the tale. You will find that they love to help you tell the story, and this becomes an opportunity to strengthen their sequencing skills. Many children who are shy and will not respond to a direct question will enthusiastically help you if you're "lost" in a story. By keeping the focus on you, the child listeners reach out with their voices and energy to help you tell the tale. So about the time you come to the first ladybug, you could try this:

Bill: So the ladybug pulled the mouse

and

The mouse pulled the kitty

and

The kitty pulled the—

[PAUSE]

Oh, the kitty pulled the—

[PAUSE]

Children: Doggy!

Bill: Right! The kitty pulled the doggy and

The doggy pulled the—

[PAUSE]

Children: Boy!

Bill: Yeah! And the boy pulled the girl

and

The girl pulled—

Children: Grandma

Bill: OK and Grandma pulled—

Children: Grandpa!

Bill: Right! And Grandpa pulled the—

Children: Turnip!

Bill: And together they pulled and pulled and pulled

But **[PAUSE]**

Bill and Children: They could not pull that turnip out!

Depending on age, you can involve the children in helping you through all or part of the sequence. You can try a variety of places to "forget" what animal comes next. Let the children's response be your guide.

 LITERACY CONNECTION: Children actively "helping" you tell a story builds their **narrative sequencing skills** as they experience the joy of assisting you in remembering the story.

Activity: The Transformation Game (Pre-K–Grade 1)

After retelling "The Big Turnip," gather the children in a circle around the pot again.

Bill: Last time each of you added a vegetable to our stew. Then we got out my cookbook. [Sometimes the children pull out their own cookbooks to add their own funny ideas!] We added three shakes of Va-va powder and four leaves from the Lopteropta tree. Now let's see. [Laughter escapes from book.] The book says, "After one week, add four shakes of Bazhunghi powder" [or any name you think is funny]. [By adding a new ingredient, you get all the children focused on the activity.]

Bill and Children: Shake-a, shake-a One. Shake-a, shake-a Two. Shake-a, shake-a Three. Shake-a, shake-a Four!

Bill: [Reading from cookbook] "Now, have each child take a taste of the stew and turn into any animal he or she wants to be. Each animal should move around the circle one (or two) times and find its place again. Then the next friend will have a turn."

Stirring the stew, stirring the stew

Take a taste. What happens to you?

[Continue until everyone has had a turn. The children love this game and will want to return to it.]

The Skeleton for "The Big Turnip"

1. Grandma and Grandpa decide to make a vegetable stew.

2. Grandpa goes to the garden to gather vegetables.

3. Grandpa cannot pull out the big turnip.

4. Grandma comes out and offers to help.

5. Together they pull.

6. **They could not pull that turnip out!**

7. A girl offers to help pull.

8. Now it's Grandpa, Grandma, and the girl pulling.

9. **They could not pull that turnip out!**

10. A boy offers to help pull.

11. Now it's Grandpa, Grandma, the girl, and the boy pulling.

12. **They could not pull that turnip out!**

13. A dog offers to help pull.

14. Now it's Grandpa, Grandma, the girl, a boy, and a dog pulling.

15. **They could not pull that turnip out!**

16. A kitty offers to help pull.

17. Now it's Grandpa, Grandma, the girl, a boy, the dog, and the cat pulling.

18. **They could not pull that turnip out!**

19. A mouse offers to help pull.

20. Now it's Grandpa, Grandma, the girl, a boy, the dog, the cat, and a mouse pulling.

21. **They could not pull that turnip out!**

22. A ladybug offers to help pull.

23. Now it's Grandpa, Grandma, the girl, a boy, the dog, the cat, a mouse, and a ladybug pulling.

24. **They could not pull that turnip out!**

25. Another ladybug offers to help pull.

26. Now it's Grandpa, Grandma, the girl, a boy, the dog, the cat, a mouse, the ladybug, and the other ladybug pulling.

27. **They could not pull that turnip out!**

28. Another ladybug offers to help pull.

29. Now it's Grandpa, Grandma, the girl, a boy, the dog, the cat, a mouse, the ladybug, another ladybug, and another ladybug pulling.

30. With all of them working together …

31. POP! Out came the turnip!

The End

Creating Cumulative Tales (Grades 2–4)

Before creating their own cumulative stories, the children should understand how they are structured. Using the stories that you have just shared, collect observations from the children about the tales. You may not need to tell all these stories for them to begin to see the structure of these tales. Choose the stories that you enjoy the most. Then begin collecting the children's observations. If it seems an additional story will clarify an idea, share another of the tales or go back to one they've already heard. If you repeat the elements listed each time a new one is added, you will have created a cumulative tale! Ask questions that allow the children to explore the stories rather than try to answer you correctly. Sometimes a child will offer an idea for an element based on one story that doesn't hold up for the others. However, he can be commended on his contribution and you can use his observation to examine and reflect on the definition of a cumulative tale. Write on a board or large paper the elements that make up a cumulative tale. A discussion might go like this:

Bill: Well, we've shared a few cumulative tales. What have you noticed about them? Are there things that are alike about all of them?

Child: They had animals in them.

Bill: Let's look at that idea. Did "Sparrow and Crow" have animals?

Children: Yes!

Bill: Did "Magpie and Milk" have animals?

Children: Yes!

Bill: Did "The Big Turnip" have animals?

Children: Yes!

Bill: So all three cumulative tales had animals. But could you have a cumulative tale without animals?

Children: Yes! [You can explore this further if you wish.]

Bill: So let's write on our chart, "Cumulative tales often have animal characters." What else?

Children: There are many characters!

Bill: Did all the stories have many characters?

Children: Yes!

Bill: Do you think all cumulative tales have many characters?

Children: Yes!

Bill: So let's write on our chart, "Cumulative tales have many characters."

Continue this discussion by collecting observations and examining them to see if they apply to the one cumulative tale or to cumulative tales in general. Add them to your chart. By the end of your discussion your chart might look like this:

- Cumulative tales may have animal characters.

- Cumulative tales have many characters.

- Cumulative tales add one character at a time.

- Cumulative tales name all the other characters every time a new character is added.

- The first character is trying to accomplish something in cumulative tales.

- The last character makes the story change in cumulative tales.

 LITERACY CONNECTION: Creating an elements chart describing a type of tale involves children in noting similarities and differences in stories and putting those observations together to build their own **understanding of narrative.**

After making a cumulative elements chart, it's time to create a group cumulative tale. There are many ways to get these tales started. Here are a couple.

Activity: Making a Cumulative Sandwich Story

 LITERACY CONNECTION: Creating a cumulative tale as a group reinforces the understanding of the **structure** of the tale, builds **narrative skills,** and encourages the group's **oral tradition.** As the group creates more and more stories together, this tradition becomes more apparent.

Bill: Let's make a cumulative sandwich. What do you start with when you make a sandwich?

Children: Bread!

Bill: OK. Our first character will be the bread. What do we want on our sandwich? [Hands shoot up.]

Children: Mayonnaise.

Bill: OK. So now we spread our mayonnaise on the piece of bread. What's next?

Children: A slice of chicken.

Bill: All right. So now we have chicken and mayonnaise on a slice of bread. What's next?

Children: An elephant ear!

Bill: An elephant ear?

Children: Yes.

Bill: OK. And now … [Hands go up. Someone calls out. Once you have accepted something out of the ordinary, you will often find the children energized to be part of the story making. As long as the suggestion fits the structure of what you're exploring and does not involve cursing or abusive language, why not use it? You have their participation!] We have an elephant's ear and chicken and mayonnaise on a piece of bread. What's next?

Children: Tomato!

> **Bill:** All right, now we have—
>
> **Children:** A buzzard's beak!
>
> **Bill:** Wait a second. Before we add anything new, what do we have to do in a cumulative tale?
>
> **Children:** Name all the characters that are already there.
>
> **Bill:** [The children's enthusiasm has given you an opportunity to reinforce the structure of this type of tale. It stays within the story creating and so has everyone's attention.] Right. So we have …
>
> **Bill and Children:** A tomato, an elephant's ear, a slice of chicken, and mayonnaise on a piece of bread.
>
> [This continues until you have a huge sandwich, and then you will probably add another piece of bread for the other side. Now it's time to explore endings.]
>
> **Bill:** Now we could just keep making this sandwich bigger and bigger, but would that make a great story? What do you see on the chart we made that talks about an ending?
>
> **Children:** [Reading chart] "The last character makes the story change in cumulative tales."
>
> **Bill:** Right, so what do we do?
>
> **Children:** Have a giant come and eat the sandwich!
>
> **Bill:** That's a cool idea. Plus it adds a new kind of character! Any other ending ideas?
>
> **Children:** The mom calls the kid in for lunch, but the dog eats the sandwich first.
>
> **Children:** The dad knocks the sandwich on the ground.
>
> **Children:** The sandwich runs away.

On and on. The energy created by keeping this an oral activity permeates the whole group. Although in some story-generating activities, it's good to move student to student sequentially, for this kind it is better to follow the impulses of the individual contributors. These individuals pave the way for the others, and creative energy can be the driving force. That being said, be on the lookout for an imaginative glisten in the eye of a child who might not be waving her hand in your face and call on her for an idea.

The sandwich-making activity is a good way to understand the building of a cumulative tale. However, the sandwich tale is not so much a story as an accumulation (another good word to use during this exploration) of elements. It really becomes a story when you add the ending. After making the cumulative sandwich, you and the children can create a more story-driven cumulative tale. Again, there are hundreds of ways to start. Here's a simple one:

Activity: Creating a "Down in the Hole" Story

Bill: Let's start another cumulative tale. One day there was a [ask children to name an animal].

Children: A beaver!

Bill: OK. Once there was a beaver walking down the road and it fell into a hole. "Help, help!" cried Beaver. Along came a—?

Children: Rabbit!

Bill: OK. Along came Rabbit. It saw Beaver in the hole and Rabbit called out, "I'll help you, Beaver!" But in a cumulative tale, can the second character solve the problem?

Children: No. There have to be more characters.

Bill: So what happens to Rabbit?

Children: It falls in, too!

Bill: And now we have Beaver and Rabbit down in the hole crying, "Help, help!" Down the road comes—?

This continues by adding more and more characters that try to help but fall in the hole. With creative questioning, you can elicit details from the children to enrich the story. You can ask how each character attempts to rescue the others. You can ask for a description of each animal—color, size, name, and how it is traveling (hopping, running, driving a car).

Or

You can create the basic outline of the story first and then add the detail. This allows you to be sure the children understand the structure before embellishing it.

Just as with the cumulative sandwich, at a certain point you have to find an ending. So:

Bill: Now we have Beaver and Rabbit and Squirrel and Kitty and Bear and Whale down in the hole crying, "Help, help!" Let's have one last character.

Children: Elephant!

Bill: OK. Along comes Elephant—

Children: She puts her trunk down the hole and they all climb up.

Bill: Other endings?

Children: The elephant falls in the hole and crushes them all!

Children: Elephant fills up the hole with water from its trunk and they all float up.

Children: The elephant walks on by.

A wonderful aspect of creating these stories is for the children to see how a story can have many endings. This oral exploration is helpful for them when creating stories or reading them.

 LITERACY CONNECTION: Considering possible endings for a story requires thinking about the characters in the story, how the action is moving, and what the story is saying thematically. It builds **narrative skills.**

Writing a Cumulative Tale (Grades 3 and 4)

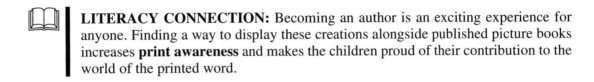 **LITERACY CONNECTION:** Becoming an author is an exciting experience for anyone. Finding a way to display these creations alongside published picture books increases **print awareness** and makes the children proud of their contribution to the world of the printed word.

If you want to add a written story to your exploration, this is a good time to do it. The children are primed by having created the group cumulative tales. They have experienced the multiple endings and know that they can follow their own imaginations. The children who are feeling less adventurous can use the "Down in the Hole" story as a model and make it their own. You can even point to alternative ways of using the "Down in the hole" model:

Bill: You can write your own version of the "Down in the Hole" story if you wish. Could you also do a similar story called "Up in a Tree"?

Children: Yes! Or "Stuck on the Moon!" or "At the Bottom of the Sea."

Children: Or we could do one like Magpie who goes to different characters!

Bill: Right.

As suggested in earlier chapters, you can divide the children into groups and have each write and illustrate a cumulative tale. You might prefer to have each child create his/her own. The stories can be a single page or many pages with multiple illustrations. They can be gathered together in a single volume or made into unique picture books. In my work with Jackie Pine and Early Stages, we have found that a story-starting page with a simple outline is helpful for some children. A copy of the story-starting page follows.

The Name of My Cumulative Tale Is

_____

by _____

It looked like this:

First I have character A: _____

Now Character B _____ is added. Now we have B _____ and A _____.

Now Character C _____ is added. Now we have C _____, B _____ and A _____.

Now Character D _____ is added. Now we have D _____, C _____, B _____ and A _____.

Now Character E _____ is added. Now we have E _____, D _____, C _____, B_____ and A _____.

Now Character F _____ is added and changes things

_____

_____

_____

_____

LITERACY CONNECTIONS: Creating circumstances for children to participate in a cumulative tale by moving, singing, and creating original stories reinforces their understanding of **narrative structure.** Understanding one story structure paves the way to noticing, exploring and understanding others.

Cumulative tales show up as stories, games, and songs in many cultures. Cumulative story games include the one about the guy named Charlie who works in a button factory and "Suitcase." Cumulative songs include "The Old Woman Who Swallowed a Fly," "The Green Grass Grew All Around," and "Bought Me a Cat." Although some of the stories from this book are not as tightly structured as the cumulative tales in this chapter, they are worth looking at and discussing as cumulative tales. These include "The Fly's Castle" (Chapter 1), "The Farmer's Noisy House" (Chapter 1), "The Talking Yam" (Chapter 6), and "The Wild Cherry Tree" (Chapter 8).

Thematic Picture Book Suggestions

LITERACY CONNECTION: Print motivation: Children will be drawn to explore picture books of cumulative tales following the work in this chapter. It will fortify their understanding and enjoyment. Here are some possibilities.

Aardema, Verna. *Bringing the Rain to the Kapiti Plain.* Puffin Books, 1983.

McCafferty, Catherine. *The Gingerbread Man.* American Education Publishing, 2001.

Taback, Simms. *The House that Jack Built.* Viking Juvenile, 2002.

Taback, Simms. *There Was an Old Lady Who Swallowed a Fly.* Viking Juvenile, 1997.

Williams, Linda. *The Little Old Lady Who Was Not Afraid of Anything.* Harper Trophy, 1988.

Chapter 14
Circle Stories

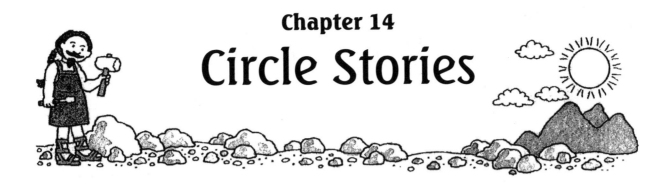

The circle story shows up in folktales from around the world. It is found in movies, songs, literature, and everyday life. Becoming familiar with the circle story structure in the folktales presented here helps children recognize it in other forms of expression or in combination with other story structures. A circle story is one that starts and ends at the same place ("place" can mean a location, a feeling, an action, or a circumstance). There are two kinds of circle stories that the boys and girls should be made aware of: the one-cycle circular tale and the repeating cycle. This chapter's opening finger play, "The Stonecutter," is a one-cycle tale in which the main character goes through a series of events and changes to end up at the same place, although with a new understanding as a result of the journey. The picture book and old favorite "The Magic Fish" is also a one-cycle circle story.

The repeating-cycle story is one in which the same series of events and actions happens over and over again. The fact that the series never stops is often part of the point of the story. The finger play "The Tomorrow Monkeys" (see Chapter 11) is a good example of this kind of circle story. Day and night, the seasons, the repetition of the days of the week, the school's schedule, the caterpillar to butterfly transformation—these are all examples of the repeating-cycle circle story.

For the creation of circle stories, this chapter focuses on the one-cycle tale.

Finger Play Warm-Up

After the warm-up, invite the children to join you in making the action and sound of the hammer and chisel: "**Chuunk, chunk, chunk,** "**Chuunk, chunk, chunk.**" You may notice a questioning look on a child's face. It is likely that someone will be uncertain of what a chisel is. Usually one or more of the other girls or boys know and can give a good definition.

 LITERACY CONNECTION: Looking to the children for definitions gets them involved in the process of building their **vocabularies.**

Once the term is clarified, you can begin the tale.

The Stonecutter

A Folktale from Japan

Once there was a Stonecutter.
Every day, **he cut stone from the mountain with
his hammer and chisel:**
**"Chuunk, chunk, chunk,
Chuunk, chunk, chunk."**

Then he lifted the stone and put it in his cart.

He cut more stone:
**"Chuunk, chunk, chunk,
Chuunk, chunk, chunk."**
Then he lifted the stone and put it in his cart.

All day, every day, the Stonecutter worked, cutting
stone and stacking it in his cart.

Every day, the sun rose and crossed the sky, shining
down on the Stonecutter. The sun made him hot.

One day the Stonecutter was very tired, and when the
sun rose and beat down on him, he felt very weak.
**"Oh, I wish I was as powerful as the sun.
I wish I were the Sun!"**

It so happened a mountain spirit was nearby.
It heard the Stonecutter and gave him his wish.
The Stonecutter became the Sun!

"Oh, I like this," said the Stonecutter who was now
the Sun. "I can see everything. I am the most powerful
thing there is!"

He was happy being the Sun until one day
a cloud floated in front of him.
"Hey! Excuse me, Cloud, I'm trying to see!"
The Cloud did not move.
"Excuse me, Cloud!"
The Cloud still did not move.
"Oh, I get it," exclaimed the Stonecutter.

The Cloud is more powerful than the Sun.
"Oh, I wish I were a Cloud!"
And, just like that, **he became a Cloud!**

The Stonecutter loved being a Cloud.
He could float across the sky, rain on gardens and
thunder when he was angry.
It was great until one day when he was trying to float
east and **the wind came at him.**

"Hey, Wind, stop! I'm trying to go the other way!"
cried the Cloud.
But the Wind did not stop.
"Oh, I get it," he exclaimed.
"The Wind is more powerful than the Cloud.
Oh, I wish I were the Wind!"
And just like that, **he became the Wind!**

The Stonecutter loved being the Wind.
He could go everywhere and see everything.
He knew he was finally the most powerful –
that is, until the day **he hit the Mountain.**

"Hey, move out of my way. I'm the Wind!"

But the Mountain did not move.

"Oh, I get it," he exclaimed.

"The Mountain is more powerful than the Wind.

Oh, I wish I were the Mountain!"

And just like that, **the Stonecutter became the Mountain!**

"Now I am truly powerful." And so it seemed.

The sun beat down and that felt good.

The clouds rained on him and cooled him off.

Then one day **he felt something at his foot—**

the foot of the mountain.

"Chuunk, chunk, chunk,

Chuunk, chunk, chunk."

"Ouch, that hurts! Hey, down there, what are you doing?

Who is that? A Stonecutter! Oh, I get it!" he exclaimed.

"The Stonecutter is more powerful than the Mountain.

Oh, I wish I was a Stonecutter again!"

And just like that, **he was a Stonecutter again.**

And he went happily back to work:

"Chuunk, chunk, chunk,

Chuunk, chunk, chunk."

The End

Storytelling Tips (All Ages)

When you tell of the mountain spirit granting the stonecutter's wish, consider adding "with three claps." Say, "It heard the Stonecutter and gave him his wish with three claps!" and then say to the children listeners, "Ready?" They will join you as you clap three times. The three claps trigger the transformation. This provides another opportunity for the children's physical involvement in the story. By using the three claps for each succeeding transformation, the children's claps move the story forward. They often like it so much that the three claps appear in their stories for whatever transformation they devise.

Depending on the age of listeners, the time of day, and how long they have been sitting, you can expand the story with descriptions of what the stonecutter can do as each new character. It can add detail, humor, and a bit more emotion because the expanded narrative pulls the listeners into each new character. It is also clearer why he becomes upset with the next obstacle. For example:

Stonecutter as Sun: Oh, this is great. I love being the sun. I can shine down on the whole earth. I can warm people up. I can make things grow. I can watch a soccer match. (Just then a cloud floated in front of him.) Hey Cloud, get out of my way; I'm watching this soccer match! Hey, didn't you hear me?! I'm the powerful sun. Now move on! Oh I get it; the cloud is more powerful than the sun. Oh, I wish I were a cloud. (Three claps!)

Activity: Acting out the Story (Pre-K–Grade 1)

One of the really great things about acting out this story is that everyone gets to be all the characters! Everyone starts out as the Stonecutter and then makes the various transformations. On occasion one (or more) of the children wants to be the spirit in the mountain and do the three claps.

Before announcing that everyone can be the stonecutter, let each child tell you her or his favorite character. By now, if they have been acting out stories with you, they know they will get to be one of the characters. This means that they will already be thinking in that direction. Letting them tell you what they want to be acknowledges their entry points to the story. Then you can move to everyone being the stonecutter.

Remind everyone of the rules:

1. Listen to the Storyteller!

2. Be safe!

3. Have fun!

When retelling the story for acting out, you might want to begin with the stonecutter in his house near the mountain. Then the children can enact the stonecutter waking up, brushing his teeth, and eating breakfast before going to work on the mountain.

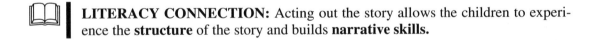 **LITERACY CONNECTION:** Acting out the story allows the children to experience the **structure** of the story and builds **narrative skills.**

Activity: Mapping out The Circle Story (Grades 2–4)

Talk briefly about "The Stonecutter" being a one-cycle story. In my work with Jackie Pine and Early Stages, we have found that mapping out the changes on a circle helps the students see how the story is structured, as shown on the next page. The reproducible page can also be used later when the students map out their own stories. Some students like to write the changes next to the numbers on the circle itself. Others prefer to fill in the blanks. Show the circle and have the students note the changes: #1 Stonecutter, #2 Sun, #3 Cloud, #4 Wind, #5 Mountain, and back to #1 Stonecutter.

My Circle Story
Is Called

_____

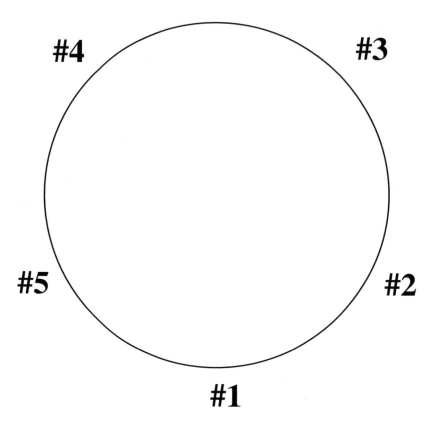

#4   **#3**

#5   **#2**

#1

My story begins at _____ #1.

It moves to _____ #2.

Then it moves to _____ #3.

Next it moves to _____ #4.

The next step is _____ #5.

And back to #1 _____ .

LITERACY CONNECTION: Mapping the **structure** of a story supports visual learners as they begin to **comprehend** how this type of story works. It also supports **narrative skills.**

Then we move on to another, a bit more complicated circle tale from Russia.

A Good Trade?

A Russian Folktale

Once there was a little old man and a little old woman. They had been married for a very long time and were still best friends and sweethearts. They lived in a little house in the middle of the woods near a river. One day, the little old man decided to take a walk. His wife asked, "You have a little money just in case?" The old man reached into his vest pocket. It was empty. He thought about it and said, "I have nothing, but I don't need anything. I'm just taking a little walk!"

So the little old man walked out the door, down the steps, and through the gate. Soon he was enjoying his morning walk in the woods. Suddenly he heard someone crying, "Help! Help!" The cry was coming from the river. The old man hurried to the water's edge. A man had fallen into the river, and the strong current was pulling him downstream. The little old man quickly picked up a tree branch lying on the ground and held it out for the drowning man to grab. Soon the man was safe on the riverbank.

"Thank you, thank you!" he said to the little old man, "You saved my life. Please join me for lunch at my house."

The little old man was hungry and quite pleased to walk with the grateful man to his home. The man, who was a merchant, had a big, beautiful house and served the old man the fanciest lunch he had ever eaten. It was delicious! After lunch, the merchant gave the little old man a chunk of gold for saving his life. It was as big as a horse's head! The little old man said, "Thank you, thank you for your generosity!" The merchant replied, "Thank you for saving my life!" The little old man picked up the big chunk of gold and started home.

As he was walking he met a man leading a magnificent black horse. The two men stopped to say hello.

"What have you there?" asked the horseman.

"A chunk of gold. I saved a man from drowning and he gave it to me," replied the little old man.

The horseman looked at the gold. The gold would make him rich. He wanted it and made an offer, "I'll trade you this magnificent horse for that chunk of gold." The horseman knew the gold could buy a dozen new horses, so he hoped to trick the old man.

The old man thought for a moment. His wife simply loved horses. "That's a good trade," exclaimed the old man. "I'll do it!" He handed the horseman the chunk of gold and proudly walked away with his magnificent new horse. He was happy. His wife would adore this handsome black horse.

Soon the little old man met a cowherd. "Where did you get that magnificent horse?" asked the cowherd. "I traded a chunk of gold for this magnificent horse," replied the old man.

"Well, I'll trade you my best milking cow for that horse," suggested the cowherd. The cowherd knew the horse was worth three cows but hoped to trick the little old man. The old man thought about the milk and cream they could have. He could almost taste the sweet butter on his wife's delicious freshly baked bread. The little old man looked at the cowherd and exclaimed, "That's a good trade; I'll do it!"

The little old man walked amongst the cows and found the healthiest one in the bunch. Leading his new cow with a rope, the little old man continued on his way home. Soon he met a shepherdess with a flock of sheep. They greeted each other, and the shepherdess asked, "Where did you get that beautiful cow?"

"I traded a magnificent horse for this beautiful cow."

The shepherdess wanted the cow and said, "I'll trade you my wooliest sheep for that cow." She knew the cow was worth five sheep, but she hoped to trick the little old man.

He thought about the warm sweaters and blankets he and his wife could have from the sheep's wool. He remembered the cold winters. So he said, "That's a good trade; I'll do it!" The little old man picked the wooliest sheep, tied his rope to its collar, said goodbye to the shepherdess and continued down the road.

He had not walked far when he met a peddler with a pack on his back. "Where did you get such a wooly sheep?" asked the peddler.

"I traded a beautiful cow for this wooly sheep."

The peddler looked at the wooly sheep and said, "Look at these strong, shiny sewing needles. I'll trade you my strongest needle for that wooly sheep." The old man thought of how his wife loved to sew, and sometimes complained about needles that bent or broke. "That's a good trade; I'll do it!" said the old man. He handed the sheep's rope to the peddler, and picked a very strong needle. He carefully put the needle in his vest pocket. The old man and peddler waved goodbye and the little old man walked on.

Soon he was at his gate, but the gate was stuck; so the little old man climbed over the fence. The needle fell out of his pocket and into the grass. The old man frantically searched through the grass for the lost needle. "Oh, no! Oh, no!" he cried.

His wife ran out on the porch and watched. "What's wrong?" she asked.

He stared at the grass and shook his head, "I lost it! I lost it," he said. "What did you lose?" asked his wife, "You left home with nothing at all."

The old man looked at her, "I know, but I've had quite a day. I saved a drowning man!"

"Good for you," said his wife, "What happened?"

"Well," said the little old man, "After I pulled him from the river, the man invited me to his home for lunch. Then he gave me a chunk of gold as big as a horse's head."

"That's wonderful!" exclaimed the little old woman. "And that's what's lost in the grass?"

The little old man smiled, "Oh, no, no, no. The gold isn't in the grass. I traded the gold!"

"You traded the gold?" asked the old woman.

"Yes," answered the old man, "I traded it for a magnificent black stallion. I know how you love horses."

"Oh my sweet husband, you traded a big chunk of gold for one horse?" she exclaimed. "Well, I do love horses! Is it lost in the grass?"

The little old man replied, "No, no, no. The horse isn't in the grass. I don't have the horse anymore. I met a cowherd and traded the horse for a beautiful cow. I knew we could use the milk and cheese and butter."

The little old woman looked at her husband, "You traded a magnificent horse for one cow?" she exclaimed in disbelief. "And the cow is lost in the grass?"

"No, the cow? It's not in the grass. You see, I traded the cow for a wooly sheep."

"A beautiful cow for one little sheep? Well," she said, "I guess we can use a wooly sheep. Its wool will make sweaters and blankets! Is the sheep lost in the grass?"

"No, no, the sheep is not in the grass. You see," said the little old man. "I had the chance to trade it for a good strong needle, and I knew you could use a nice strong needle. I made a good trade, but it fell out of my pocket when I climbed over the fence. I'm sorry. I hope I can find it!" He began looking through the grass again.

The old woman watched her husband searching for the needle. "Oh, leave it, dear," she said, "You've done more than enough today already. I'm not so sure about your trades, but I do know I wouldn't trade you for the world! I'm glad you're home. Come inside and let's have supper."

The little old man looked at his wife, smiled, and said, "I wouldn't trade you for the world either!" Then he followed her into the house.

The End

~telling Tips (All Ages)

As presented, "A Good Trade?" is a very elaborately told story. Still it's sometimes fun to add more detail about the wealthy man's house. Although it may seem complicated, basically it is a pretty simple tale. If you follow the skeleton for this story, you will find that you can include details that have stayed with you or ones that your own imagination supplies when retelling the tale.

This tale is told in a number of cultures. It appears in collections of both British and Norwegian tales. In the British version, the old woman gets really angry with the old man, calls him a fool, and beats him.

Activity: Mapping out the Story (Grades 2–4)

 LITERACY CONNECTION: Repeating the activity of mapping out a story builds **narrative skills** and shows the children they can apply this technique to many stories. If it doesn't fit the circle map, they discover that it is not a circle story. Your dialogue can become a model for an internal dialogue.

With the children, map out the circular path this story takes. Having mapped out "The Stonecutter," the children's first impulse may be to name the first character mentioned in the story. Here's a possible exchange:

Bill: Let's map out this story. What shall we put at the #1 position?

Children: The old man!

Bill: If #1 is the old man, what is #2?

Children: [think about it, shake heads] Then it's not the old man; it's the gold.

Bill: If #1 is the gold, what is # 2?

Children: The horse!

Bill: And when we make it all the way around the circle, we come to …?

Children: Not the gold. He winds up with nothing in his pocket.

Children: Just like he started! #1 is nothing! #2 is the gold. And so on.

Now you can map out the story with #1 being "nothing."

The Skeleton for "A Good Trade?"

1. There are an old man and old woman.

2. The old man has nothing in his pocket.

3. The old man goes for a walk.

4. The old man saves a drowning man.

5. The drowning man is rich.

6. The rich man invites the old man home.

7. The rich man gives the old man chunk of gold.

8. The old man trades gold for horse.

9. The old man trades the horse for a cow.

10. The old man trades the cow for a sheep.

11. The old man trades the sheep for a needle.

12. The old man loses the needle climbing over a fence.

13. The old man searches for the needle in the grass.

14. The old woman comes out of their house.

15. The old woman asks the old man step by step what happened.

16. After the old man reveals that he started with gold and wound up with a needle lost in the grass, she says to come inside.

17. Neither would trade the other.

The End

Activity: Mapping the Story from a Picture Book (Grades 2–4)

After mapping out "The Stonecutter" and "A Good Trade?," you might want to share a picture book like "The Magic Fish" (see end of chapter for a version of this tale). Use the circle and map out the changes that occur in this story, starting with the rustic house. Sometimes the children suggest that the fisherman or the fish should be #1. Following is a potential dialogue:

Bill: We have just read the circle story **The Magic Fish.** If we map it out on our circle, what will be #1?

Children: The fish.

Bill: If the fish is #1, what would be #2?

Children: [after thinking about your question] I'm not sure. Maybe it's not the fish.

Bill: What else could it be?

Children: The hut.

Bill: Then what would be #2?

Children: The little cottage.

Bill: Does that work?

Children: Yes!

From there the group can map the rest of the story. Some circle stories require more than five stops, a notion they will discover.

Creating Circle Stories (Grades 2–4)

 LITERACY CONNECTION: Creating circle stories as a group allows children to use their understanding of the **structure** for their own creation. It contributes to their **narrative skills** and to the group's **oral tradition.**

After sharing and mapping out the preceding stories, it is time to create some circle stories. As with the other chapters in this section on the structure of stories, it is good to start with a structure for which the children supply the characters and details. The following story offers an exciting premise that the children will be eager to add their own contributions. In fact, you will probably never tell the story as it is written, because it is designed to substitute the children's ideas for those suggested in the text. This method is an exciting one for the boys and girls because they hear their ideas becoming part of the story. These ideas ignite the other children's imaginations and they are ready to add to the next opening in the tale. Second graders enjoy this story-making activity as well, but for them the creation of an original circle story requires a lot of support. Third and fourth graders can create circle stories on their own after you have guided them through the stories and activities in the chapter.

Changing Jobs

There was once a librarian who worked with children. She helped them find books. She read about new books and ordered ones she felt the kids who came in would enjoy. She ran programs with authors and storytellers visiting the library. She liked the job, but she wanted something different. She decided she'd like to be a doctor.

So she became a doctor. She loved being a doctor, taking care of people and working in a hospital. She loved it until the day she had to operate. She could not handle cutting through somebody's skin. So she decided to become a farmer.

So she became a farmer. She loved living in the country and getting up early every morning. She liked the hard work in the field. She was certain this was the perfect job until the tornado came. The tornado picked up her house (with her in it!) and carried it five miles and dropped it into a lake. Luckily she could swim, but she was done with farming. She decided to be a firefighter.

So she became a firefighter. She loved the firehouse, the firedog, the slide-down pole, and the fire engine. She was a good driver, so she got to drive a lot. There was only one problem with this new job. She was afraid of fires! So she decided to become a rock-and-roll star.

So she became a rock-and -roll star. She loved the costumes and being on stage. She loved singing and playing guitar. Everything was great until she tripped over an electric guitar cable and fell off the stage. As she lay on the floor, she got to thinking about the library. She thought about the children and the new books and the authors she got to meet.

The next morning she was back at the library and was pleased as can be. There was a new book that had just arrived. Its title was *Home Is Where the Heart Is*.

The End

Activity: Creating the "Changing Jobs" Story with the Children (Grades 2–4)

The story "Changing Jobs" is a lot more fun if you let the children suggest the jobs and why the jobs were abandoned. It might go like this:

Bill: There was once a librarian who worked with children. She helped them find books. She read about new books and ordered ones she felt the kids who came in would enjoy. She ran programs with authors and storytellers visiting the library. She liked the job but she wanted something different. She decided she'd like to be ——— (Look around)

Children: A movie star!

Bill: OK. So the librarian became a movie star, and she loved it. She had a beautiful house in Hollywood. But then one day— [To children] What happened that made her want to leave?

Children: The director wanted her to kiss Frankenstein!

Bill: OK. And she said, "Forget it. I quit." So then she became [you will see the hands raised now—everyone wants to contribute to this story].

Children: A doctor!

Bill: As a doctor she loved making people feel better. It was great until the day—

This continues as long as you wish.

Sometimes, the children have an idea for the next job before anyone has suggested a reason she left the present job. With third and fourth graders, it's important to slow that momentum and focus on the reason she decided on a change. Describing an event that causes her to leave makes the story more compelling. It also involves the students in noticing and making choices that they all agree improves the story. At some point in the process, remind everyone that the story must come to an end. Mention that the structure of the story suggests what that ending will be.

> **Bill:** After all, what kind of story is this?
>
> **Children:** A circle story!
>
> **Bill:** So what does she need to become?
>
> **Children:** A librarian again!
>
> **Bill:** Why?
>
> **Children:** She misses the books!
>
> **Children:** She misses the kids!

Note: It's interesting how many children like the idea that the librarian misses the children—often the very same ones who called out at the beginning, "She quit being librarian because she was sick of kids!"

LITERACY CONNECTION: Having the children explore a variety of endings supports **narrative understanding,** makes them more aware of endings in general, and makes their ongoing story encounters more meaningful.

Activity: Creating Other Group Circle Stories (Grades 2–4)

Before setting up writing teams or the individual storywriters, it's fun to do another simple story creation as a group. Here are a few launch ideas. Just as with the "Changing Jobs" story, ask the students to give reasons for moving on. Create a group circle story about one of these or an idea you or one of the children suggest:

- Deciding what to wear to a special event (a hat, a coat, a dress, a costume)

- Finding a new home (could use a person or an animal)

- Painting your house

The students may come up with their own ideas for launch places. You can follow one or more of them or suggest those ideas be saved for writing.

Activity: Creating and Writing a Circle Story (Grades 3 and 4)

LITERACY CONNECTION: Writing a circle story is the next big step in this process. The children will exercise their **narrative skills,** and appreciate that their stories belong to a great tradition of a particular type of tale, the Circle Story.

The group stories as well as the folktales in this chapter now serve as models for their own creations. Many of the children will write a story that is similar to one of the ones they heard. I used to worry about their lack of originality, but as I thought more about it, I realized that they were demonstrating a grasp of the structure. Retelling a tale requires recognition of the structure of the story. Many stories contain elements from other stories. Folktales have traveled and changed from country to country and yet still come from the same stories. This is what is happening here, and it is a good experience for the children. Those that use the structure to explore their own creative ideas are children who have found a special relationship to creative writing and this activity allows them to flourish as well.

After sharing the stories and creating circle stories as a group, the children will be excited to get their ideas down on paper. Many will find it helpful to use the Circle Story Circle to map out their story before they write it. As in the preceding chapters in Part Four, they can write alone or in small groups. They can use multiple illustrations and pages to create a picture book or a single illustrated story to be compiled into a volume of Circle Stories.

Other Circle Stories in this Book

Although some of the following stories are not as tightly structured circle stories as the ones in this chapter, they are worth looking at and discussing. They include "The Farmer's Noisy House" (Chapter 1), "The Calabash Children" (Chapter 4), "The Wild Cherry Tree" (Chapter 8), "The Tomorrow Monkeys" (Chapter 9), and "Why the Moon Gets Smaller" (Chapter 12).

Thematic Picture Book Suggestions

 LITERACY CONNECTION: Print awareness and **print motivation.** The following books can accompany the stories the children have already enjoyed. They may want to map out some of these stories and place them alongside the books they have created.

Burns, Marilyn, and Gordon Silveria. *The Greedy Triangle.* Scholastic Press, 1995.

Joffe Numeroff, Laura, and Felicia Bond. *If You Give a Mouse a Cookie.* Laura Geringer Publisher, 1985.

Littledale, Freya, and Winslow Pels (illustrator). *The Magic Fish.* Scholastic, 1987.

McDonald, Margaret Read, and Nancy Dunaway Fowlkes. *The Old Woman Who Lived in a Vinegar Bottle.* August House, 1995, 2003.

Myers, Tim, and Oki S. Han (illustrator). *Basho and the River Stones.* Marshal Cavendish, 2004.

Resources

Africa

A'Bodjedi, Enenge. *Ndowe Tales 1*. Ndowe International Press, 1999.

Appiah, Peggy, Anthony Appiah, and Ivor Agyeman-Duah (editors). *Bu Me Be: Akan Proverbs*. Africa World Press, 2003.

Courlander, Harold. *A Treasury of African Folklore: The Oral Literature, Traditions, Myths, Legends, Epics, Tales, Recollections, Wisdom, Sayings, and Humor of Africa*. Marlowe, 1996.

Greaves, Nick, and Rod Clement, *When Hippo Was Hairy*. Barron's, 1990.

Arctic

Goodchild, Peter (editor). *Raven Tales*. Chicago Review Press, 1991.

Norman, Howard. *Northern Tales*. Pantheon Books, 1990.

Asia and the Pacific Islands

Courlander, Harold. *The Tiger's Whisker and Other Tales From Asia and the Pacific*. Henry Holt, 1995.

de Souza, Eunice. *One Hundred and One Folktales from India*. Penguin Global, 2005.

Eberhard, Wolfram. *Folktales of China*. University of Chicago Press, 1968.

Sakade, Florence (editor), and Yoshisuke Kurosaki. *Japanese Children's Favorite Stories*. Tuttle, 2003 (third rev. edition).

Spagnoli, Cathy. *Asian Tales and Tellers*. August House, 1998.

Australia

Green, Gracie, Joe Tramacchi, and Lucille Gill. *Tjarany Roughtail: The Dreaming of the Roughtail Lizard and Other Stories Told by the Kukatja*. Magabala Books, 2000.

Morgan, Sally. *The Flying Emu and Other Australian Stories*. Alfred A. Knopf, 1993.

Caribbean

Berry, James. *Spiderman Anancy.* Henry Holt, 1998.

Sherlock, Philip. *West Indian Folktales.* Oxford University Press, 1989.

Turenne Des Pres, Francois. *Children of Yayoute: Folktales of Haiti.* Universe Publishing, 1994.

Wolkstein, Diane. *The Magic Orange Tree and Other Haitian Folktales.* Schocken Books, 1978, 1997.

Central and South America

Bierhorst, John (editor). *Latin American Folktales: Stories from Hispanic and Indian Traditions.* Pantheon Books, 2002.

Brenner, Anita, and Jean Charlot. *The Boy Who Could Do Anything & Other Mexican Folktales.* Linnet Books, 1992 (reprint edition).

Brusca, Maria Cristina, and Tona Wilson. *Pedro Fools the Gringo and Other Tales of a Latin American Trickster.* Henry Holt & Company, 1995.

Despain, Pleasant, and Mario Lamo-Jimenez. *The Emerald Lizard: Fifteen Latin American Tales to Tell in English and Spanish.* August House, 1999.

Dorson, Mercedes, and Jeanne Wilmot. *Tales from the Rainforest.* Ecco Press, 1997.

Europe and the British Isles

Asbjornsen, Peter Christen, Jorgen Engebretsen Moe, and George Webbe Dasent. *East O' the Sun and West O' the Moon* (59 Norwegian Tales). Dover, 1970.

Clavino, Italo. *Italian Folktales.* Harvest/HBJ Book, 1992.

Crossley-Hollan, Kevin. *Folktales of the British Isles.* Pantheon, 1988.

Pourrat, Henri. *French Folktales.* Pantheon, 1989.

Segal, Lore (translator), Maurice Sendak (illustrator), and Randall Jarrell (translator). *The Juniper Tree and Other Tales from Grimm.* Farrar, Straus & Giroux, 2003 (revised edition).

Yeats, William Butler. *Treasury of Irish Myth, Legend & Folklore.* Gramercy, 1988.

General

Cole, Joanna. *Best Loved Folktales of the World.* Doubleday, 1982.

Pelowski, Anne. *Drawing Stories from around the World and a Sampling of European Handkerchief Stories.* Libraries Unlimited, 2005.

Rosen, Michael. *South and North, East and West.* Humanities Press, 1992.

Stern, Anita. *World Folktales.* McGraw-Hill, 2001.

Middle East

Muhawi, Ibrahim, and Sharif Kanaana. *Speak, Bird, Speak Again: Palestinian Arab Folktales.* University of California Press, 1989.

Schwartz, Howard. *Miriam's Tambourine: Jewish Folktales from around the World.* Oxford University Press, 1988.

North America

Bruchac, Joseph, and Murv Jacob. *The Boy Who Lived with the Bears and Other Iroquois Stories.* Parabola Books, 2003.

Chase, Richard. *The Jack Tales.* Houghton Mifflin, 2003.

Hamilton, Virginia, Leo Dillon (illustrator), and Diane Dillon (illustrator). *The People Could Fly: American Black Folktales.* Knopf Books for Young Readers, 1993 (reprint edition).

Hayes, Joe. *The Checker Playing Hound Dog: Tall Tales from a Southwestern Storyteller.* Mariposa, 1986.

Pijoan, Teresa. *White Wolf Woman.* August House, 1992.

San Souci, Robert D. *Cut from the Same Cloth: American Women of Myth, Legend, and Tall Tale.* Putnam, 2000.

Russia

Avery, Gillian, and Ivan Bilibin, *Russian Fairy Tales.* Everyman's Library, 1995.

Riordan, James. *The Sun Maiden and the Crescent Moon: Siberian Folktales.* Interlink Books, 1998.

Index

The Author's Work

Bill Gordh has been working with storytelling and young children for many years. A substantial part of his work in early childhood curriculum has been developed at The Episcopal School in the City of New York where he is the Director of Expressive Arts. He has also had residencies and led workshops in many other early childhood programs. The Storytelling/Creative Writing curriculum Bill developed with Executive Director Jacqueline Pine at **Early Stages** has taken him to a variety of public schools for residencies working with 2nd and 3rd graders. (Chapters 11–14). He also has a yearly residency at the Tribeca Learning Center (PS 150) where he works with Pre-K through 3rd graders. The summers find Bill exploring this work with educators as a co-director of the Manhattanville College School of Education's **Summer Arts Institute.**

©JohnKraus 2006.

Bill has also been published extensively, having over three dozen articles appearing in a variety of educational journals including the cover story in Scholastic's **Early Childhood Today** and in a series on children's literacy in **Sesame Street Parents** magazine. Two of Bill's early readers published by Golden Books and Random House have sold over 200,000 copies cumulatively. His ongoing explorations in the power of story recently led to a commission to create a new work for the **New York Philharmonic's Young People's Concert Series**. The collaboration with the composer **Jon Deak** culminated in the world premier of **The Roaring Mountain** that took place at Avery Fisher Hall on April 2, 2005 in New York City. Bill is consultant and host of storytelling for the **Tribeca Film Festival Family Day.** Other venues for his storytelling work have included **The Museum of Natural History, The New York Historical Society, The Museum of American Folk Art**, **The Byzantine Chapel Fresco Museum** and for three years he was a featured storyteller at the **White House Easter Egg Roll.** His **Lingonberry Music** recordings have received several national awards including the ALA Notable Recording. Bill lives in New York City with his wife and two children.